Values and Valuation in the Practice of Educational Administration

Donald J. Willower
Joseph W. Licata

CORWIN PRESS, INC.
A Sage Publications Company
Thousand Oaks, California

For information:

Corwin Press, Inc.
A Sage Publications Company
2455 Teller Road
Thousand Oaks, California 91320
E-mail: order@corwin.sagepub.com

SAGE Publications Ltd.
6 Bonhill Street
London EC2A 4PU
United Kingdom

SAGE Publications India Pvt. Ltd.
M-32 Market
Greater Kailash I
New Delhi 110 048 India

Printed in the United States of America

Library of Congress Cataloging-in-Publication Data

Willower, Donald J.
    Values and valuation in the practice of educational administration / authors, Donald J. Willower and Joseph W. Licata.
        p.   cm.
    Includes index.
    ISBN 0-8039-6631-8 (cloth: acid-free paper).
    —ISBN 0-8039-6632-6 (pbk.: acid-free paper)
        1. School management and organization—Moral and ethical aspects —United States—Case studies. 2. Social values—United States— Case studies. 3. Decision-making—Moral and ethical aspects—United States—Case studies. I. Licata, Joseph W., 1942- . II. Title.
    LB2805.W526   1997
    371.2—dc21   97-4720

This book is printed on acid-free paper.

97 98 99 00 01 02 03 10 9 8 7 6 5 4 3 2 1

Editorial Assistant:	Kristen L. Gibson
Production Editor:	Diana E. Axelsen
Production Assistant:	Denise Santoyo
Typesetter/Designer:	Lisa Liddy
Indexer:	Virgil Diodato
Cover Designer:	Marcia R. Finlayson

Contents

Preface

This book is, to our knowledge, the first in educational administration that deals with values and valuation as both philosophical
and practical problems. A philosophical view of values and valuation
is presented that serves as a grounding for reflective moral decision
making. A variety of specific cases is used to connect the processes of
ethical choice to concrete situations. Most work on values in educational administration neglects valuation. We emphasize valuation since
it provides a way of proceeding for those facing ethical problems or
dilemmas. Consequence analysis, the effort to foresee the likely outcomes of given courses of action, is a key feature of our approach. We
believe our approach is practical and useful to those facing moral
choices. We argue that without this practical, concrete side, ethics
remain merely abstract. We have shared the problems of teaching
valuation and consequence analysis because we believe both instructors and students can benefit from the experience, and we do not like
the idea of a guide for instructors only, especially given the subject

matter of this text. The book can be used in different ways. Either the philosophical approach or the cases can be given greater emphasis, while the other gets relatively less but enough to show the inter-relation of the two. Furthermore, we have tried to include cases of various kinds and of varying complexity to fit the needs of different teaching situations. We are fully aware that using valuation and con-sequence analysis in making moral choices is something administra-tors will have to work at, and we also recognize that there can be many a slipup along the way. Still, most savvy educational adminis-trators are tired of fleeting fads and panaceas. They understand both the difficulty and the importance of making morally justifiable choices. We hope our work will be helpful to them.

About the Authors

DONALD J. WILLOWER is Distinguished Professor of Education at The Pennsylvania State University, based in the Department of Education Policy Studies. He has served there as chair of the Educational Administration Department, acting head of the Division of Education Policy Studies, and acting dean of the College of Education.

An army veteran, he received the B.A. and M.A., both in philosophy, and the Ed.D in general administration from the University at Buffalo, where he taught in both the Department of Philosophy and the School of Education. In Buffalo, he headed a personnel agency in the private sector and was employed in that city's public schools.

He was a Kellogg Fellow in educational administration and the social sciences at the University of Oregon, served on the National Commission on the Preparation of School Administrators of the American Association of School Administrators, was twice elected to the Board of Trustees of the University Council for Educational Administration, including a term as president, and was a member of its National Commission on Excellence in Educational Administration.

His research and writing have dealt with schools as organizations and philosophical issues in educational administration. He has authored more than 170 publications on these topics, two of which received Davis awards for best publication in *Educational Administration Quarterly*. He has presented invited papers in various settings including Panama, Australia, and Brazil, and has been a consultant to universities, school systems, and governmental agencies, here and overseas.

JOSEPH W. LICATA is Professor of Education at Oklahoma State University where he has served as head of the Department of Educational Administration and Higher Education. He has served as head of the Department of Administrative and Foundational Services and associate dean of the College of Education, Louisiana State University. He also served with the academic faculty in educational administration and as a senior faculty member with the Mershon Center for Education and Research in National Security and Policy Sciences at The Ohio State University. His three degrees include the B.S. from the University of Connecticut, the M.S. from Glassboro State College (NJ) and the Ph.D. from The Pennsylvania State University.

Beginning his career in education as a public school teacher and principal, he has combined this experience with subsequent study and research to develop two state-wide internship projects for school administrators in Georgia and Louisiana. His is coauthor and author of numerous publications that deal with schools as organizations and the design and implementation of problem-solving initiatives for practicing school administrators. Recent recognition for his research includes the W. G. Walker Award for the best paper in the *Journal of Educational Administration*, 1995. His former graduate students hold positions in the public schools, state education agencies, and higher education.

• 1 •

Introduction

Administrative Work and Quick Fixes

The work of administration is political and frequently rife with conflict. Most administrators are engaged in a variety of brief, fragmented, and often interrupted activities on a daily basis. They face varied and sometimes contradictory expectations from a diversity of individuals and groups, some having special interests or axes to grind. They also are a focal point for gossip and secrets and are privy to the foibles, eccentricities, and the often humorous goings-on in their organizations.[1]

Above all, administration is concerned with values. Values can be defined as conceptions of the desirable, and administrators regularly make choices from among competing conceptions of the desirable. In choosing between competing values, sometimes it is a matter of electing to move forward with one program rather than another when both are good ideas but resources are scarce. Sometimes it is a matter of choosing between the lesser of two evils when circumstances require such a decision. Sometimes the decision will be to do nothing for the time being, if all the options are undesirable and waiting does not have serious drawbacks.[2]

The human element is pervasive, and some individuals or groups may be disappointed, annoyed, or even seriously disaffected by particular decisions and what they perceive to be a direction that the organization is taking. Furthermore, unhappy members of the organization might feel that the source of their difficulties is the administrator.

Clearly, the complexities, contingencies, and pressures of administration can be daunting, and many practitioners are ready to consider any measures that might be helpful. To be sure, there has been no shortage of help. There have been wide-ranging and ongoing efforts by researchers to understand the behavior of organizations and the individuals who participate in them. As with all scientific endeavors, these efforts at best have resulted in explanations or theories, many of which have substantial empirical support. However, all theories are tentative and uncertain, even those representing the best available knowledge. More to the point for administrators, the implications of theories for particular decisions have to be thought through and worked out by those applying them.

This is not easy to do. Personal predilections and biases, past experiences, lore, perceived pressures, and a variety of other idiosyncratic elements often play a large part in decision making. Beyond that, over the years, a multitude of quick fixes and panaceas have been offered to administrators by those wishing to help or to profit from the nostrums they dispense. Many of these quick fixes have some elements that are reasonable and useful. However, they are frequently marketed as large-scale packages with numerous principles and procedures that make it easier to sell materials and consulting services. Some of these fixes are associated with a particular person who becomes a kind of guru for advocates and adherents.

In sharp contrast with more scientific endeavors, these commercialized efforts are ordinarily not very modest about their claims for success. Indeed, such claims are commonly part of the sales pitch. Although there might actually be some small successes, a more noteworthy outcome is likely to be a cadre of believers. Some, especially those with a stake in the success of the particular remedy, will be true believers, whereas others will be temporary believers. After all, new nostrums will appear, new bandwagons will be created, and the current fix will become passé. Administrators who want to be associated with the new remedy, including some who like to be seen as using the latest regimen, whatever it might be, will jump on the new bandwagon.

The history of administration amply documents the popularity of quick fixes and panaceas; almost anybody interested in administration and organizations can name the latest two or three. All this is readily understandable, it fits the conditions of administrative work: the complexities, contingencies, and pressures cited earlier. It also fits the contexts within which organizations operate: the disparate pushes for goal attainment and economy of resource allocation faced by both public and private sector institutions. Small wonder that administrators, who may feel personally responsible for their organization's fate, should be attracted by the possibility of quick fixes, not to mention the influence of others who might view the failure to adopt a particular remedy as a shortcoming.[3]

Most packaged remedies consist of small grains of insight scattered on larger seas of dogma that typically fail to recognize the complexities of administration. Oversimplified recommendations are common. To give just one example, participative decision making is often advocated. In and of itself, this idea is attractive and sensible. However, its implementation is usually quite complex. Just what decisions should be participative? Who should participate? What should be the modes of participation? Do people act as individuals, experts, or representatives of particular groups or interests? Do they contribute by providing feedback, advising, or voting? In what decisions do various individuals and groups want to participate? Which ones do they prefer to leave to others? How can participative decisions be directed toward larger purposes than the special interests of the participants? These are just some of the questions that can be asked.

The answer to such questions is, "It all depends." This is not a very satisfactory answer, but it is an honest one. It depends on the particular circumstances in that setting and on what is sought by those involved. Put differently, implementation depends on the realities of the situation and the values of the participants. Prepackaged programs ignore such contingencies.

It would simplify life considerably if there were easy and certain answers for every question. The truth is that there are not. Many of the remedies, slogans, proverbs, and other bits of advice offered administrators, however they are presented, could be harmless, but sometimes they are misleading, and usually they are not very effective. Being involved in a packaged program might leave some people feeling better (although it can work both ways) and might generate helpful self-fulfilling prophecies, but there are great costs such as oversimplification and dependency on a pregiven set of answers rather than depending on the intelligent use of a variety of concepts and ideas relevant to the specifics of the situation. Stated another way, quick fixes ignore complexity and drive out thinking.

Toward Thoughtful Practice

There are no panaceas in life or in administration. The recognition of this fact can be the beginning of a more thoughtful and more practical kind of administration. Aristotle and other Greek philosophers wrote about practice that is informed, deliberate, and purposeful. Their term, *praxis*, is used to refer to thoughtful practice. Such practice is the antithesis of both personal predilection and the packaged quick fix.

It is striking that this concept of practice from around the 4th century B.C. should be so relevant to current administration. Indeed, a reasonable contemporary approach to administration would have to emphasize the same kinds of things: a concern about purpose or values, a deliberate process of analysis, and information in the form of relevant concepts and explanations. One of the principal differences between ourselves and the Greek philosophers is that we have the advantages of the results of many years of scientific work. Today, relevant knowledge about organizations and their administration can be found in the social sciences and their allied fields.

The purpose of this book is to present a practical approach to administration that is philosophically sound and scientifically informed. Because the practice of administration is concerned with values, we argue that administrators require not only a well-developed set of commitments but also a workable process of valuation that will enable them to make informed choices between competing values. Furthermore, we see knowledge about how things are likely to work as essential to such choices, if they are to be wise ones.

Next, we examine briefly the situation in the literature of educational administration relevant to values and administrative practice. We then present a general philosophical position with an integrated view of values, practice, and science. Included is a discussion of the process of valuation as it applies to concrete situations in administration. After that, we discuss some of characteristics of school organizations along with the problems and opportunities they can present for administrators trying to move their organizations toward more desirable futures. This discussion occurs in the context of the problems of internalization and institutionalization. The former deals with the problem of making thoughtful practice habitual for the individual; the latter deals with integrating the processes of deliberation and thoughtful practice into the routines and everyday life of the organization.

The remainder of the book is composed of vignettes, cases, and exercises that can be used in a practical way by administrators and those who teach administration. Issues in the use of these materials are explored. Our intention is to make the processes of valuation and choice as clear and as available as we can, with an eye to the concrete problems of the practicing administrator.

Having taken special note of the complexities and pressures of administrative work, we want to emphasize its robustness, challenges, and significance. Administration can be exciting, fun, and rewarding, and it can affect the lives and prospects of others. We should try to use the best ideals, methods, and ideas available. Recognizing that mindless commitments to panaceas and quick fixes are unlikely to help and could be harmful, we should also recognize that all attempts to improve organizations, even when using the best means available, will be chancy and fallible. But that is simply part of the human condition, it adds spice to life and to administration. Although our examples and referents are to educational organizations and their administration, the philosophic position and the processes set forth apply to all kinds of organizations as well as to the problems of everyday living.

Notes

1. Studies of administrator work that focus on the allocation of time and attention often follow some version of the methods proposed by Henry Mintzberg, *The Nature of Managerial Work* (New York: Harper & Row, 1973). For citations to a number of these studies and some criticisms, see D. J. Willower, "School Organizations: Perspectives in Juxtaposition," *Educational Administration Quarterly* 23 (1982): 89-110. On humor and some of the oddities of administration, see C. T. Burford, "Humor of Principals and Its Impact on Teachers and the School," *Journal of Educational Administration* 25 (1987): 29-54; T. R. Kippeny and D. J. Willower, "Humor, Peers and the School Superintendent," *Administrator's Notebook* 34 (1990): 1-4; P. W. Jackson, "Lonely at the Top: Observations on the Genesis of Administrative Isolation," *Administrator's Notebook* 25 (1977): 1-4.

2. The definition of values given here has fairly wide usage. See, for example, the chapter by Clyde Kluckholn et al., "Values and Value Orientations in the Theory of Action," in *Toward a General Theory of Action*, ed. T. Parsons and E. A. Shils (Cambridge, MA: Harvard University Press, 1951). On values as an emerging area of greater importance in educational administration see D. J. Willower, "Synthesis and Projection," in *Handbook of Research on Educational Administration*, ed. N. J. Boyan (New York: Longman, 1988). On decision making see S. Estler, "Decision Making," *Handbook of Research on Educational Administration*, ed. N. J. Boyan (New York: Longman, 1988). A classic on decision making is H. A. Simon, *Administrative Behavior* (New York: Macmillan, 1958).

3. A good source on various approaches to organization theory and the movements sometimes associated with different schools of thought is Charles Perrow, *Complex Organizations: A Critical Essay* (New York: Random House, 1986). See also Perrow's article, "The Short and Glorious History of Organization Theory," *Organizational Dynamics* 2 (1973): 2-15.

An Associated Press story in the popular press recently listed and discussed a variety of management fads. Included were downsizing (small is beautiful) and conglomerating (big is beautiful), management by walking around, quality and "all those theories that poured out of Japan," strategic planning, empowerment, and the maxims touted in books such as the *One Minute Manager* and others.

Educational administration is influenced by many of the fads from business administration. Some school administrators seem to believe that using practices from business will give them and their organizations greater legitimation. The total quality craze is a good example of this belief. In addition, the schools face an array of quick fixes associated with teaching that are periodically issued from commissions, "experts," politicians, special interest groups, and assorted others with programs they hope to promote.

• 2 •

Values

Past Views and Recent History

Some Past Views

Philosophers have traditionally explored values as part of larger ethical perspectives. Today, much of what was formulated is respected for its contribution to the history of thought, but it is often seen as having limited relevance to contemporary problems of ethics and values. To cite just a few of the classic thinkers, Plato's *idea of the good* was the highest of his ideal forms. The forms were held to transcend temporal phenomena and to be immutable and real. Aristotle believed that rationality was the distinctive human characteristic and saw its cultivation in a life of contemplation and moderation as good. Spinoza contended that a good life was attained through the intellectual love of God, defined pantheistically and identified with nature. Kant's categorical imperative stated that one should act as if that action were to become a universal law. Jeremy Bentham's touchstone in ethics was the greatest happiness of the greatest number. Nietzsche saw the society of his day as dissolute and envisaged a "superman," above the human herd, living a creative life of heroic morality unfettered by the good and evil of conventional moral precepts.

More recent philosophers have been concerned with issues such as the proper grounding of ethical principles and have continued the discussions of the good, virtue, justice, and values that have been the historical hallmarks of the study of ethics. The place of the state in human affairs has been part of ethics since the time of the Greek philosophers. However, the importance of this topic has been enhanced because of concerns about individual freedom, justice, and equity within the context of an array of social problems made more vivid than ever before by the pervasiveness of mass media.

Recent History

Although few would deny that the questions explored by philosophers are of great significance because they are fundamental ones, the answers provided often seemed too abstract or one-sided to be definitive in making choices from among competing values. Hence, it is not surprising that broad-gauged approaches to ethics have not played a significant part in the exploration of values in administration.

There is no question that values have become more salient in recent years in the literature of educational administration, but the field has been oriented to values virtually from its inception. One of its earliest scholars, W. T. Harris, was the long-time editor of the *Journal of Speculative Philosophy*. He was an authority on Hegel and an educational administrator as well, serving not only as a school superintendent but also as U.S. Commissioner of Education. Both Harris and W. H. Payne, who is credited with writing the first book on school administration, were interested in advancing a more scientific approach to education, but both were also committed to the key place of ideals. Indeed, this was true of many of the best scholars in the field from Ellwood Cubberley to Paul Mort.[1] Despite the influence of such individuals, the literature of the field remained largely hortatory, often featuring the pronouncements of prominent school officials and educators on the problems of the day. Neither science nor philosophy was a definitive influence, although both were used and promoted by various individuals and groups.

All this began to change in the 1950s with major efforts to profes-sionalize scholarship and preparation in educational administration. The use of social science concepts and theories became commonplace rather quickly as various professional associations and university groups recognized their relevance to the problems of administrators. After all, the work of these public officials was conducted mainly with people in individual, organizational, and community contexts; the social sciences clearly could offer much that was germane to un-derstanding behavior in such settings.

This change led to a torrent of research and theorizing and to increased specialization among scholars, often along the lines of so-cial science disciplines. A variety of social science theories and methods were employed, and much was learned in such areas as schools as organizations and the politics and economics of education. From the 1950s through the 1970s, much of the energy of the best scholars in the field was devoted to such research.[2] During that period, philoso-phy and values were ongoing concerns in educational administra-tion, but this work did not even begin to approach the volume of the empirical research of the time. This is not surprising because many were mindful that much of the earlier hortatorical writing that schol-ars were now attempting to get beyond was oriented toward values, usually in a personal and unsystematic way. Also, the logical positiv-ists and others had emphasized the linguistic distinction between normative (ought) and descriptive (is) propositions.

Those interested in philosophical questions became aware that more was required than a statement of personal values. Philosophi-cal knowledge, if not training, seemed essential. This probably had a deterring influence but also a positive one because it took the sub-ject seriously. It was also taken seriously by associations such as the University Council for Educational Administration that, in the 1960s, sponsored conferences and publications on philosophy, val-ues, and the uses of the humanities in educational administration.[3]

Such concerns had not been ignored in the social sciences. Robert Lynd raised the "Knowledge for what?" question in his 1939 mono-graph of that title, the same year that Lewin and his colleagues pub-lished their studies of democratic, authoritarian, and laissez-faire leadership. The former reflected an abiding moral concern for how knowledge is used, a concern that is perhaps most vividly seen in connection with the physical and biological sciences. Lewin's work was an example of studies that explored arrangements widely deemed desirable, such as democratic administration or participative management. These studies continue today and examine whether such arrangements have positive outcomes for organizations and individuals.

Democratic administration was a particular focus in educational administration, especially in the period before and after World War II, but a host of related concepts such as participative decision making, organizational development, and various collegial styles of leadership were also touted and studied. Empowerment is a contemporary version that is getting considerable attention, often in conjunction with restructuring, which usually refers to rearranged and more inclusive decision processes, especially at the school building level. As in related work in the social sciences, the general idea in educational administration has been to study the organizational effects of such variables with the hope that there would be salutary ones.

Despite some contrary findings, it seems fair to say that participative arrangements often have positive attitudinal outcomes for those directly involved, but results related to basic organizational pursuits such as productivity in industry or student learning in schools have been far less clear, suggesting the need for finer-grained theories going beyond simple participatory formats.[4] The point to keep in mind is that some of the research done in the social sciences and in educational administration was tied to melioristic intentions. Such intentions remain powerful influences today and are readily seen in the currently popular studies of gender, race, class, and various kinds of "at risk" students, where the hope is to improve the lot of a particular group. Indeed, the idea that knowledge can be used to improve the human condition has been a common justification of science.

Critique of Science

The political and social activism of the 1960s and 1970s was fed by a distrust of social institutions. This included government, business, and among others, science. Neo-Marxists and subjectivists, for years philosophical enemies, were able to capitalize on the disillusionment of those times and moved from their previously marginal status in the social sciences and philosophy to become major players, especially on campuses and especially in fields in the social sciences and the humanities. The student activism and various reformist movements of the period gave these views a prominence that they

had not enjoyed before. Both became strong, indeed nearly domi-
nant in, for example, sociology.[5]

Eventually, the ferment in these fields reached educational
administration, where, in the 1970s and 1980s, first subjectivism and
then the critical theory version of neo-Marxism became noteworthy
strands of thought and criticism. The substance of these views has
been chronicled elsewhere.[6] For our purposes, the main points to keep
in mind are the following. Subjectivists criticized science as devoted
to objectivity while ignoring values and humanistic considerations.
Critical theorists saw science as a political force shaped by the ruling
classes to promote their own interests. Both argued that values
(although each promoted a different set of values), not scientific
work, should be the central focus of the field. Subjectivists emphasized what they saw as humanistic principles, and critical theorists
emphasized social justice for the underclasses through a realignment
of power relations in the society.

Rejoinder

A crucial limitation of both of these views was that their rejection
of science cut them off from the very sources that could facilitate the
attainment of change and growth in the direction of valued and improved futures. Put simply, science is necessary to thoughtful valuation. If we are to improve the human condition, even in the small
ways open to us, it helps if we have insights into how things are
likely to work. In addition, the skeptical features of science are
important to the critical assessment of judgments of desirability,
something missing in the political agenda of neo-Marxists and in the
odd combination of absolutism and relativism that is characteristic
of many subjectivists.[7]

Although critical theorists and subjectivists both presented flawed
views, their emphasis on the importance of values found fertile soil in
educational administration because it was shared by virtually everyone. A prolonged debate resulted. The real issues went beyond the
importance of values to the substance of values and to the matter of
valuation. Which values should be stressed and what processes
should be employed in making ethical choices were the questions
that required attention, although the latter had been ignored by critics
of both views.

It appears that today, neo-Marxism and subjectivism have run their course and are waning in social sciences such as sociology. Alexander attributes the decline to their one-sidedness and to the radical and polemical character of their views, which he sees as giving way to a more balanced, more synthetic kind of theorizing. For some years now, educational administration has reflected trends in sociology. It may do so in this case as well, although the applied character of educational administration sets it off from fields such as sociology.

In any event, alternatives to critical theory and subjectivism are increasingly being put forward.[8] We will present a philosophical view that speaks in a practical way to the moral issues faced by administrators. It is not our intention to continue the debates that have marked the literature in educational administration, so we have kept our history of the debates on values in the field as brief as possible, although we consider and reject some of the positions taken by critical theorists, subjectivists, and others in our treatment of valuation.

For those who wish to read directly the views of critical theorists and subjectivists, a number of sources have been provided in the notes. These sources also cite numerous other writers in the same camps. Fuller treatments of our criticisms of these views are also cited. Our position is that an adequate conception of values and valuation requires an adequate conception of inquiry and science. This is the topic we turn to next.

Notes

1. On the history of thought in educational administration see R. F. Campbell, T. Fleming, L. J. Newell, and J. W. Bennion, *A History of Thought and Practice in Educational Administration* (New York: Teachers College Press, 1987); J. A. Culbertson, "A Century's Quest for a Knowledge Base," in *Handbook of Research on Educational Administration*, ed. N. J. Boyan (New York: Longman, 1988).

2. A great deal of this research is summarized and discussed in the 32 review chapters in N. J. Boyan, ed., *Handbook of Research on Educational Administration*.

3. See, for example, R. E. Ohm and W. G. Monahan, eds., *Educational Administration: Philosophy in Action* (Norman: University of Oklahoma, 1965); R. H. Farquhar, *The Humanities in Preparing Educational Administrators* (Eugene, OR: ERIC Clearinghouse on Educational Administration, State-of-the-Knowledge Series 7, 1970). UCEA was involved in both of these publications. The earlier, landmark book sponsored by the National Conference

(now Council) of Professors of Educational Administration, employed a number of social science concepts but it also contained a chapter on values. See O. B. Graff and C. M. Street, "Developing a Value Framework for Educational Administration," in *Administrative Behavior in Education*, ed. R. F. Campbell and R. T. Gregg (New York: Harper, 1957).

4. See R. S. Lynd, *Knowledge for What?* (Princeton, NJ: Princeton University Press, 1939). A well-known early study of democratic leadership was K. Lewin, R. Lippitt, and R. K. White, "Patterns of Aggressive Behavior in Experimentally Created Social Climates," *Journal of Social Psychology* 10 (1939): 271-301. Democratic administration is discussed extensively in R. F. Campbell et al., *A History of Thought and Practice in Educational Administration*. On the organizational outcomes of participative arrangements, see G. A. Yukl, *Leadership in Organizations* (Englewood Cliffs, NJ: Prentice Hall, 1989).

5. See J. C. Alexander, "The New Theoretical Movement," in *Handbook of Sociology*, ed. N. J. Smelser (Newbury Park, CA: Sage, 1988).

6. See D. J. Willower, *Educational Administration: Inquiry, Values, Practice*, rev. ed. (Lancaster, PA and Basel, Switzerland: Technomic, 1994). This work gives the main arguments and counterarguments in connection with critical theory and subjectivism. The various sources, including the works of critical theorists and subjectivists, are cited there. See also C. W. Evers and G. Lakomski, *Knowing Educational Administration* (Oxford, England: Pergamon, 1991) and D. J. Willower's review pieces, "Educational Administration: Intellectual Trends," in *Encyclopedia of Educational Research*, 6th ed., vol. 2., ed. M. C. Alkin (New York: Macmillan, 1992) and "Administration of Education as a Field of Study," in *International Encyclopedia of Education*, 2d ed., vol. 1, ed. T. Husen and T. N. Postlethwaite (Oxford, England: Pergamon, 1994).

7. A recent source on a leading subjectivist writer in educational administration is T. B. Greenfield and P. Ribbins, *Greenfield on Educational Administration: Towards a Humane Science* (London: Routledge, 1993). This is a collection of many of the papers of Greenfield who died in 1992.

8. The reference to Alexander is to "The New Theoretical Movement." To give just a few examples of recent writing on values in educational administration, see L. G. Beck, *Reclaiming Educational Administration as a Caring Profession* (New York: Teachers College Press, 1994). As its title suggests, the book presents caring as its central focus and draws, in part, from feminist literature. T. J. Sergiovanni, *Moral Leadership* (San Francisco: Jossey-Bass, 1992), deals with ethics and leadership. Christopher Hodgkinson has written three books on ethics in the subjectivist tradition. If Greenfield was that movement's polemicist in educational administration, Hodgkinson was its more systematic ethicist. His latest book is *Educational Leadership: The Moral Art* (Albany: SUNY Press, 1991).

· 3 ·

Values
Philosophical Context

Values Without Valuation

That so much attention could be given to values in educational administration, but so little to the process of valuation, seems incongruous. Part of the explanation is that neo-Marxian critical theory and subjectivism both stem from traditions that do not emphasize the place of deliberation and judgment in ethics. Both have their array of preset values: The radical left has its political program, these days often couched in the rhetoric of emancipation and entitlement, and subjectivists often subscribe to the notion of a values hierarchy that typically culminates in absolute principles.[1]

Not only did these views de-emphasize concrete moral choices among competing values, something at the heart of nonroutine administrative decision making, but adherents of both views in educational administration made scathing attacks on school officials. For example, a critical theorist argued that organizations such as schools regulate access to knowledge in ways that favor some groups and exclude others and charged that school administrators abet or cope with this situation rather than attempt to change it. A leading subjectivist depicted administrators as dehumanized technocrats who detach themselves from their decisions, which they then justify as selfless and objective.[2]

The censorious language and nature of these attacks suggest that they are seen by those making them as part of their critical polemic against what they perceive to be the mainstream point of view. Supporting data are not presented. What is presented are the stereotypes that fit the positions of the critic. Critical theorists hope to replace their stereotype—the administrator as cat's paw of the ruling classes—with administrators (and teachers) who are radicalized "culture workers" devoted to the emancipation of the oppressed underclasses. Subjectivists are harder to pin down, but their stereotype—the administrator as technocratic, robotlike decision maker—is to be replaced by empathetic, sensitive, humane individuals. Of course, even while rejecting the unfair stereotype, most of us would applaud the latter list of characteristics. Both groups no doubt see their replacements as devoted to moral principle. However, in ethics, a problem arises when lists of desirable characteristics or of moral principles are taken as independent and absolute, then are discovered to conflict with one another in real situations. For example, honesty and compassion sometimes conflict; a textbook example of conflict is whether one should steal or even injure another to obtain food for one's starving children.

When a clear-cut, agreed-on principle stands alone, the decision is an easy one, but abstract principles cannot always be decisive. The difficult cases come when there are competing goods, the kind of thing administrators sometimes refer to as the "gray areas" or the "tough ones."

Real situations teach us that what at first appears to be an easy decision sometimes has negative effects or unexpected consequences. They also teach us that important problems tend to have complex rather than simple solutions. Most decisions have at least some negative consequences that may not be foreseen without attention to the concrete circumstances at hand. Looking at the particulars moves the locus of moral choice from the abstract to the existential, to things that really make a difference to those involved.

History is full of examples of the dominance of abstract moral codes conjoined with the neglect of specific instances of manifest injustice; a great deal of immorality has been perpetuated in the name of morality. The separation of ethical deliberation and judgment from concrete situations can result in moral ritualism in which professed commitment to a moral code substitutes for the effort to behave in a moral way. Putting this another way, the separation of values from valuation can make morality a mere abstraction.

Ethics and Philosophy

The view of valuation we present is an integral part of our position on ethics, and our position on ethics is embedded in a general philosophy. Essentially, in the broad tradition of philosophical naturalism, our position draws on Dewey's instrumentalism and especially his conception of inquiry.[3] However, true to the spirit of naturalism and free inquiry, on particular issues, we take the position that we feel is most warranted by logic, the available evidence, and whatever reason and wisdom we are able to muster. Furthermore, our ultimate focus is organizations and their administration, topics that have traditionally not been emphasized in philosophy.

Philosophy in Educational Administration

In the philosophical debates in educational administration, our position is an alternative to critical theory, subjectivism, and positivism. We reject all three of those views. Critical theory, like most forms of neo-Marxism, suffers greatly from its uncritical embrace of a radical political agenda, its failure to apply standards of criticism to itself while labeling other views as mere ideologies designed to gain or keep power (a label that seems made for their own position), its incorrect assumptions about a unitary and all-controlling ruling class in what is actually an era of pluralistic politics, and its pretensions in seeing itself as speaking for the working and disadvantaged classes when its adherents are mainly intellectuals and it has little or no popular support.

Subjectivism is often faulted for being relativistic—that is, for having no criteria with which to distinguish good ideas from bad ones. Because it stresses the unique experience of individuals, it has serious difficulties with intersubjectivity and with concepts such as knowledge or society. As alluded to earlier, in ethics, subjectivists often adopt some form of transcendentalism in the style of philosophical idealism.

Positivism (in its later versions logical positivism and logical empiricism) is a dated philosophical view that has very little contemporary visibility. The term *positivism* was used in the 19th century by Auguste Comte, and the philosophy was developed much later in the 1920s and early 1930s, especially by the members of what was called the Vienna Circle. As a philosophy, it rejected metaphysics and emphasized science. Influenced heavily by the work of the physical sciences, positivism depicted propositions that could not be operationalized and measured as meaningless speculations, and it saw ethics as mere preference. Although logical positivism, and especially its logical empiricist versions, provided some useful concepts and were counterpositions to some of the more far-fetched metaphysics of the time, they were deeply flawed by their narrow conception of science and in their separation of science and values.[4]

We do not make note of our rejection of positivism because that position is a viable one today in philosophy proper. It isn't. However, positivism has been a major target for both critical theorists and subjectivists, who equate science with positivism and take aim at the latter to criticize the former. Both the critical theorists and the subjectivists attack a straw man when they depict science as mechanistic, seeking final truth, and cut off from human concerns and values. In addition, science is often blamed for technologies that have undesirable effects.

Negative and inaccurate views of science have been advanced not only by neo-Marxists and subjectivists but also by a variety of postmodernists and poststructuralists who deny reason and stress indeterminacy, as well as by some radical feminists and some advocates for particular racial, ethnic, or class groups who have argued that science is essentially a political activity and who have tried to gain support for a view of politicized science that would help to legitimate their ideological agendas.[5] These criticisms embody a distorted view of science. We turn now to a more balanced and more accurate view of scientific activity and methods. In it, we are less interested in responding to far-fetched claims and more interested in showing the value and importance of science for humanity and efforts to improve its lot.

Science

Science is a human invention and a very human enterprise. Its main activities depend on individuals who are curious about how things work, create tentative explanations, and subject those explanations to public assessment. Science is anything but mysterious or arcane. Its methods are open and well-known. A problem that may begin as an anomaly, that whets curiosity and calls for explanation, is given better definition and formulation often after extended observation. Through a process of reasoning and conjecture, a theory or explanation is devised. The theory, which itself can be thought of as a hypothesis, can be used to generate more specific hypotheses.

Hypotheses are essentially reflective speculations that eventually have to be assessed. Empirical trials of one kind or another can be used to determine whether a particular hypothesis is consistent with data gathered to test it. Important additional criteria of assessment include the logic and consistency of the explanation, its coherence with previously supported theory, and its fruitfulness as a source of testable new ideas. When an explanation meets such criteria, it gains in credibility. However, science is not a search for final truths. It does not deal with certainties. Even the most well-established theories are seen as tentative because science is self-corrective. The fate of theories is to be modified or replaced as inquirers seek out new and better explanations. John Dewey's definition of truth as "warranted assertibility" is consistent with this state of affairs. Within Dewey's naturalistic framework, assertions are warranted by evidence obtained using the best means and methods currently available.[6]

Critics argue that bias and politics are so ingrained in the human condition that objectivity is impossible and science is tainted. Postmodernists, in particular, contend that writings in the social sciences and elsewhere can be seen as sources of domination and oppression, which they believe is demonstrated when such "texts" are *deconstructed*, a vaporous term they employ to refer to analysis using their assumptions.

The argument that bias and politics are ubiquitous in human affairs is, of course, correct. That is why there are scientific norms geared to minimizing and controlling such effects. The norms of science are like all science, human constructions developed and maintained by people. They differ somewhat in emphasis by specialty, with more rigorous standards in fields where prediction and replication are most clear-cut. Across various areas of study, these norms include skeptical open-mindedness, the public communication of results, and impersonal criteria of evaluation. When scholarship fails to meet these kinds of standards, it is commonly viewed as deficient, although much leeway is given to those who are developing new ideas and to those who are explicit about the limitations of their work.[7]

Another version of the bias-politics argument is the point that observations are theory-laden and ultimately subjective. Here again we have a half-truth. Observations are theory-laden, but if such theory is thought to be distorting, there are many countermeasures, from multiple observers to the conscious use of several theories to the phe-nomenological device of bracketing presuppositions. If the theory-ladenness is explicit and intended, in the end, observations laden with some theories will turn out to be better than those laden with other theories with regard to scientific consequences or results. Science is deeply subjective in the sense that the thinking and the observation are done by people. After all, the interplay of observations and creative minds is one of the more fascinating aspects of inquiry and a basic source of interesting theory. This creative side of science is balanced by its critical side where all ideas are greeted with skepticism, and one must be willing to strive to disprove one's own theories.

Arguments made against science pale beside the history of scientific accomplishments. Airplanes fly, a variety of human organs can be transplanted, and in school organizations, the attitudes and behavior of administrators and teachers are quite predictable in important respects. That some of the technologies generated by science have been used malevolently is a sad commentary on human weakness, but not an argument that undercuts the efficacy of scientific methods or their potential for gaining knowledge and doing good.

Science in Everyday Life

The conception of science espoused here does not make a sharp distinction between the more formal sciences and everyday life. Science is inquiry that gives special attention to the processes of description and interpretation, but scientific knowledge is not fundamentally different from everyday knowledge. Nor are the social sciences seen as intrinsically different from the other special sciences. All of them are *natural sciences* in the broad sense of that term, but the social sciences are less developed than the physical or biological sciences. Although the special sciences differ substantially from one another in the techniques and regimens employed, they are all distinguished by a commitment to scientific methods and to the scientific temper and attitude that reflect the norms discussed earlier.

Scientific methods and the scientific temper can also be brought to the level of the individual, as Dewey has shown. Dewey's theory of inquiry is the centerpiece of his philosophy. It can be equated with scientific method, although Dewey often used equivalent terms such as *reflective methods* and *deliberation,* especially in connection with individuals and their efforts to resolve problematic situations.

For Dewey, much of human behavior is relatively automatic, with impulse and habit playing major roles. It is when problematic situations arise that reflective (or scientific) methods are brought into play. The problem at hand needs to be formulated, and alternative courses of action that deal with the problem need to be tried out in thought. Possible courses of action become hypotheses to be assessed reflectively for their likely consequences, both short- and long-range. Intelligent thought or reflection thus becomes an instrumentality that can lead to problem resolution. Such resolutions are never final because they invariably lead to new conditions and new problems. Preferred courses of action can be assessed to determine how well they have worked in the past, but they remain experiments in problem resolution that may or may not fit new circumstances. This kind of reflective process is at one with scientific methods, for as Dewey puts it, "scientific methods simply exhibit free intelligence operating in the best manner available at a given time."[8]

Inquiry and Ethics

In a naturalistic philosophy, inquiry and scientific or reflective methods are brought to bear on ethical problems just as they are on other kinds of problems. Issues in ethics are not separated from their concrete and empirical contexts. Doing the right thing, whether it's a matter of trying to determine a desirable future to work toward or of making a choice among competing values in a pressing current situation, depends on being able to assess and deal with the complexities of the particular circumstances at hand.

Pregiven answers of whatever kind ignore the realities and the moral subtleties found in actual moral dilemmas. Because of this, absolutes or quick fixes are not adequate substitutes for reflective assessment. As was noted earlier, genuine moral choices arise in the gray areas. When one alternative is clearly more desirable than the others, the decision is virtually routine. Reflective methods make crucial contributions in ethics precisely where they are most needed— when the choices are close or when moving toward a desirable goal is especially complex.

In administration, there are many such choices, which is one of the reasons why administrative practice is ultimately a deeply moral undertaking. In making such choices, good intentions are important, but alone they are not sufficient. A good heart is something to be desired and respected, and good-hearted individuals will likely be drawn to compassionate, humane alternatives. In administration, however, the problem ordinarily is not so much one of wanting to do the right thing as it is of actually being able to implement the right thing.

Moral Problems

It is helpful to distinguish the kind of moral problem that is thrust on administrators and the kind that administrators themselves originate. The former is the kind of problem that arises during the daily activities of the organization: a student is accused of stealing from another student; a teacher develops a personal problem that threatens to interfere with effective instruction; the parents of a student demand some form of special treatment for their child; a community group indicates unhappiness with an element of the curriculum. Received problems of this sort are common, but they are not routine in the sense that they cannot be resolved with a quick response or action. Each requires reflective attention.

The administrator-originated problem is the kind that would probably not be acted on if it were not defined as a problem by a perceptive individual or group. Quite often, such definition begins when a need or lack is noticed. Sometimes problems are formulated as part of a conscious effort to improve the organization and its services to its clients. Some examples are when teachers and administrators note a weakness in student preparation in American history and advocate strengthening that part of the curriculum; when student services are reviewed and a reorganization of pupil personnel staffing and procedures is proposed; when a committee of teachers and parents charged with making recommendations to improve their school suggests that the development of problem-solving skills and self-sufficiency become an instructional theme across classrooms and areas of study. Originated problems such as these presumably have already had reflective attention but will ordinarily require more before a final decision to move ahead.

Values, Principles, and Implementation

Inquiry into moral problems has both normative and descriptive dimensions, although these dimensions often blend into one another.

On the normative side is the issue of the relative worth of values and the topic of ethical principles. On the descriptive side is the issue of the implementation of specific courses of action aimed at choosing among competing values and attaining desirable objectives.

When it comes to the relative worth of values, there is considerable agreement on the general worth of a fairly large number of values and on the lack of worth of another fairly large number, often polar opposites of those in the former group. For example, most people would agree on the desirability of liberty, friendship, kindness, justice, learning, compassion, health, love, adventure, and curiosity. Most would agree on the undesirability of subjection, enmity, cruelty, injustice, ignorance, and so on.

Because the former qualities are usually considered in the abstract to be desirable, we call them values. The literature of ethics sometimes uses other terms such as *ideals* or *virtues*. These terms also refer to desirable qualities, although ideals sometimes suggests an element of unattainability along with desirability, and virtue is often used to indicate a desired personal characteristic. The concept of an ethical principle commonly connotes a proposition or statement that is well established. Examples might be, "Treat others with kindness," or "Be truthful." We believe that it is useful to be sensitive to the nuances of terminology; to be sure, it is essential to understanding a particular writer if he or she uses terms in an unusual way. However, one should not get bogged down in pedantry. The important thing is to be aware of and come to grips with the substance of ethics.

The terms we cited—values, ideals, virtues, and ethical principles—obviously overlap in the sense that they all are concerned with desirable qualities, dispositions, or states of affairs. An issue in ethical theory is the extent to which such qualities can be ranked and whether there are absolute values or ethical principles. In a naturalistic philosophy, ethical principles or well-established values attain their status through use and experience. They result from cumulative ethical inquiry and knowledge and they are seen as guides to ethical choice, but they are not treated as absolutes. Fixed or final principles serve to block valuation and separate ethics from realities. In addition, the quandary of absolute principles that conflict with one another in concrete situations underscores the flaws associated with absolutist views.

The list of values given earlier readily suggests the scope of such quandaries. A common one in administration is that between compassion and honesty. Another from administration illustrates a different version of the quandary, it is that giving something desirable to one person or group may mean that something desirable is taken from another person or group. Nevertheless, there is much agreement about desirable qualities and states. There is likely to be a good deal of consensus too, about the characteristics of a good person and even of a good organization. The basic problem remains one of implementation.[9]

The mention of implementation at once reminds us that holding a set of abstract values to be desirable is a far cry from actually doing something to enhance their attainment in concrete situations. The real world is a complicated and messy place that can defy our attempts to understand it, and even our best efforts, whether we call them the methods of inquiry, reflective methods, or scientific methods, will often fall short or fail.[10] The situation, in some respects, is reminiscent of Winston Churchill's famous comment that democracy is the worst form of government except for all the others that have ever been tried. So it is with these methods. They are fallible and subject to all of the slipups that can result from human limitations and situational complexities. It's just that they work better than any other methods tried to date.

Notes

1. For a call to "leftist educators" to go beyond critique and produce radicalized teachers prepared to engage in "cultural politics," see H. A. Giroux and P. McLaren, "Teacher Education as a Counterpublic Sphere: Radical Pedagogy as a Form of Cultural Politics," *Philosophy and Social Criticism* 1 (1987): 51-69. A subjectivist ethics that includes a hierarchy of values is C. Hodgkinson, *Educational Leadership: The Moral Art* (Albany: SUNY Press, 1991).

2. The attacks on administrators are illustrated from the standpoint of critical theory in R. J. Bates, "Educational Administration, the Sociology of Science and the Management of Knowledge," *Educational Administration Quarterly* 16 (1980): 1-20. Attacks from subjectivists are exemplified in T. B. Greenfield, "The Decline and Fall of Science in Educational Administration," *Interchange* 17 (1986): 57-80.

3. Dewey's conception of inquiry is found in J. Dewey, *Logic: The Theory of Inquiry* (New York: Henry Holt, 1938). See also D. J. Willower, "Dewey's Theory of Inquiry and Reflective Administration," *Journal of Educational Administration* 32 (1994): 5-22. M. Farber's naturalistic perspective

also influences our views, see *Naturalism and Subjectivism* (Springfield, IL: Charles C. Thomas, 1959).

4. Comte's (1798-1857) writings are mainly of historical interest. See, for example, *The Positive Philosophy of Auguste Comte*, trans. Harriet Martineau, 2 vols. (London: J. Chapman, 1953). For an examination of positivism and related views see H. Feigl and W. Sellars, ed., *Readings in Philosophical Analysis* (New York: Appleton-Century-Crofts, 1949). This collection includes well-known pieces taken from articles or books by authors who contributed to logical positivism and logical empiricism, including some who were part of the Vienna Circle. It also provides a good overview of strands of thought that were similar in some respects to positivism, for instance, analytic philosophy, which had important British roots and was considered by some to be a less flawed, more appealing successor to positivism.

On the current exaggeration of the influence of positivism, see D. C. Phillips, *The Social Scientist's Bestiary* (Oxford, England: Pergamon, 1992); D. J. Willower, "Educational Administration and the Spirit of the Times," *Educational Administration Quarterly* 32 (1996): 344-65.

5. Postmodernism (and its mainly French version, poststructuralism) is now making its way into writings in education. It has been applied extensively in areas such as literary studies that do not have traditions of rigorous scholarship. Some of its leading writers and examples of their work are J. Derrida, *Speech and Phenomena* (Evanston, IL: Northwestern University Press, 1973); M. Foucault, *Language, Counter-Memory, Practice* (Ithaca, NY: Cornell University Press, 1977); and J. F. Lyotard, *The Postmodern Condition* (Manchester, England: Manchester University Press, 1984). An amusing critique is F. G. Verges, "The Unbearable Lightness of Deconstruction," *Philosophy* 67 (1992): 386-93.

Those whose main focus is advocacy for a particular group, which is usually depicted as oppressed or otherwise not getting a proper share of societal regard or benefits, cannot be readily classified. For instance, some are neo-Marxists and some are anti-Marxists; however, their views share common problems. One problem is the enormous within group variation that characterizes gender, racial, and ethnic categories. Another concerns the pitfalls of exclusivity, separatism, societal fragmentation, and failure to examine the preferred group critically. It is not surprising that ethics in philosophy have focused on the individual, and sometimes on achieved characteristics, but rarely on ascribed ones. Recently, neo-Marxists, especially critical theorists, and postmodernists have adopted aspects of one another's views, sometimes mixed with features of gender or racial politics. See S. Davies, "Leaps of Faith: Shifting Currents in Critical Sociology of Education," *American Journal of Sociology* 100 (1995): 1448-78.

6. See Dewey's *Logic: The Theory of Inquiry*.

7. On norms in science, see R. K. Merton, *The Sociology of Science* (Chicago: University of Chicago Press, 1973); H. Zuckerman, "The Sociology of Science," in *Handbook of Sociology*, ed. N. J. Smelser (Newbury Park, CA: Sage, 1988).

8. The quotation is from Dewey's *Logic: The Theory of Inquiry*, 535. The discussion of science in everyday life and of the "natural" sciences draws on Dewey. One of his best works on the uses of reflective methods in concrete situations is *Human Nature and Conduct* (New York: Henry Holt, 1922).

9. On principles, see J. Dewey and J. H. Tufts, *Ethics* (New York: Henry Holt, 1932), 230. See also S. Hook, "The Place of John Dewey in Modern Thought," in *Philosophic Thought in France and the United States*, ed. M. Farber (Buffalo, NY: University of Buffalo Publications in Philosophy, 1950). D. J. Willower, "A Colleague of the Written Word," *Journal of Educational Administration and Foundations* 8 (1993): 58-61, a short piece on Christopher Hodgkinson's work, suggests that despite our disagreements over the nature of principles, on a practical level, for example, that of school improvement, there would likely be major areas of agreement.

10. The term *real world* is an interesting and an apt one in that academics often use it to refer to reality, presumably as opposed to the abstract and utopian world of their cloistered institutions. Academic freedom, properly valued because it protects inquiry and dissent, also protects dogmatic pronouncements and outlandish conclusions. We have had a lot of the latter in recent years, much of it from selected neo-Marxists, postmodernists, and special interest group advocates. The political views of such writers demonstrate the isolation of the academy. Although these views are widely disseminated within universities, especially in the humanities and social sciences, outside of it, in the "real world," they have failed to attract significant support.

·4·

Moral Valuation

Valuation in Practice

Enhancing values in actual situations involves both a sensitivity to appropriate values and ethical principles and an ability to see values as part of real-life contexts that affect the likelihood of their realization. Put differently, values are attained by implementing specific courses of action having specific consequences. Often, the courses of action proposed for implementation have probable consequences that can affect other values, sometimes negatively. That is why moral choice in administration is really a matter of *valuation*, a term we use to refer to the process of choosing from and implementing conceptions of the desirable with an awareness of and sensitivity to their potential consequences for a variety of individuals and groups, as well as the multiplicity of values typically affected by implementation.

An emphasis on valuation rather than on values alone gives life and meaning to values that are so often honored in a ritualistic manner that separates them from concrete situations. An emphasis on valuation also underscores the importance of praxis or thoughtful practice in administration, just as it exposes the futility of pregiven answers and packaged quick fixes. Examples of valuation will be presented that illustrate the kinds of problems already discussed, for example, problems that arise during the daily activities of the organization and that have to be dealt with, and originated problems that come from a deliberate effort to improve some aspect of organizational work or results. Both kinds of problems are concerned with moral choices and competing values and both are attacked using similar procedures. The main difference between them is that the originated problem is initially a product of conscious and explicit plans to achieve a particular desirable future.

The steps employed in valuation are those of ordinary scientific method applied to decision situations: a problem is formulated, alternative solutions are thought up, the probable consequences of each alternative are elaborated conceptually, and a course of action is selected that seems most likely to attain the valued outcomes sought. Because the alternatives and their consequences represent working hypotheses, the event as it actually plays out becomes a kind of experiment from which we can all learn.

Our approach differs from most other ethical perspectives in several ways. First, we believe that, to have more than inspirational meaning, ethics must be concrete and particular. Second, we emphasize scanning for desirable possibilities. We believe that individuals can affect their futures, but to do so intelligently, they must devote deliberate attention to the possibilities. Third, we stress consequence analysis as an integral and necessary aspect of ethical choice. We are especially concerned about mitigating negative consequences as part of larger ethical decisions. Fourth, we emphasize the utility of social science concepts and explanations in assisting administrators and others in their search for probable consequences and likely desirable outcomes.

In all this, we recognize the fallibility of our methods and the limitations imposed by the human condition. We realize that there can be honest disagreement about which desirable futures should receive priority. We expect that well-intended people will often make incorrect judgments about how certain valuable aims might be attained. We also recognize that unanticipated interventions can occur as events unfold, changing the circumstances that were the basis of prior deliberations. We do not argue that our methods are panaceas or free of errors, only that they are the best available in a protean, complex, and changing world. In considering valuation more specifically, we first discuss searching for desirable futures, and then discuss scanning for alternative problem solutions with special emphasis on consequence analysis using a short case. After that, we present two longer cases for illustrative purposes. Our aim is to show how valuation proceeds in the context of several different kinds of concrete problems.

Searching for Desirable Futures

The search for desirable futures is an integral part of an administration oriented to values, but it is not part of the usual routines of many administrators. Administration is work that is never complete. One can arrive on the job without a well thought out agenda of any kind and be kept busy the whole day. From the first "gotta minute?" through an array of scheduled and unscheduled meetings, telephone calls, unexpected problems and interruptions, issue adjudication, required routines, and minor and not so minor crises, to the last activity accomplished, administrators ordinarily feel they have put in a good day's work and earned their pay. Whether or not the administrator has made progress that day in moving the organization toward some desirable state of affairs is not especially relevant to this sense of accomplishment because of the many other tasks that have been completed.

Normally, administrative work is devoted to keeping things running smoothly, handling the unexpected along with the everyday tasks, listening to concerns and complaints, fielding requests, keeping crises from developing or getting out of hand, and giving reassurance and support. Activity of this kind is not only essential to organizational well-being, it also promotes a variety of values from compassion to the resolution of harmful difficulties. Although we all know that some administrators do not measure up along these lines, many are able to have effective, and essentially moral, work lives even though they do not expend time and energy explicitly searching for desirable futures.

Honorable and caring though they may be, such administrators will never know what might have been. Searching for desirable futures, after all, is simply an effort to find worthwhile possibilities. Such searches might lead to the framing of a problem that was formerly overlooked, or it might lead to the conclusion that something already being done well could be done better. This kind of search presents us with what we earlier called an originated problem. Obviously, individuals of sensitivity and vision may be able to imagine feasible future states that others do not see so clearly. But everyone can work at it and, especially for the administrators of educational organizations, the cultivation of vision that includes desirable future states is surely an obligation. After all, the beneficiaries of successful school improvement will be the students, the staff, or both.

We use the term *vision* to refer to the ability to imagine desirable future states along with possible paths to their attainment. Here, it is necessary to recognize that desirable future states, even feasible ones, are rarely fully attainable. For example, if student tolerance toward others is seen as a value that should be given additional attention, and a course of action is implemented, the result might be a major improvement but it will not be perfect. Most good things have to be continually won and rewon in everyday living. Even though what we have called vision will be imperfectly achieved, it differs greatly from being merely visionary. Vision emphasizes values but is connected to at least preliminary judgments of feasibility. Visionaries are likely to promote schemes that are essentially unworkable, often divisive, and squander energies in efforts doomed to failure. The presentation of desirable futures is the main contribution of vision. Early attention to feasibility helps to weed out futures that may be desirable but are clearly unobtainable. Futures that appear to be particularly desirable and that seem feasible can eventually be developed for more critical valuation.

The search for desirable futures can be facilitated by a variety of techniques. All techniques have the purpose of pointing to value possibilities that otherwise might be neglected. One can scan the array of values found in philosophy and other literature. We listed some values of this kind earlier. These values often are quite general, but they can remind us of values we would normally not think of and, in effect, broaden our immediate horizons. For example, one of the values on our list was adventure. This concept, used to describe activity that is challenging and elicits excitement and zest, is interesting because it is an example of an often neglected value and because so many writers over the years (not to mention students, past and present) have described schools as artificial and vapid.[1] However, the main point is not the importance of this value. The main point is that this kind of scanning, which can be accomplished quickly, is capable of calling attention to unlikely values that, on closer inspection, might be judged worthy of being incorporated in school improvement efforts.

Closer to organizational concerns (and thereby having a certain prior legitimacy) are teaching objectives of various kinds. Scanning these objectives from numerous sources, both internal and external, can reveal values that are attractive and that currently may not be receiving enough attention in the organization. Traditional objectives include the gaining of knowledge as represented by mastering certain subject matter, various kinds of social skills, problem solving and critical thinking capabilities, self-discipline and self-sufficiency, respect for the worth and dignity of every individual, and good citizenship.

A related kind of scanning focuses on organizational goals. These goals are articulated at various levels of explicitness in different organizations. Those stated for one's own organization in goal statements and planning documents are highly legitimate in the sense that they represent formally accepted aims. Often they are quite general. For instance, a relatively common goal in school organizations, stated variously, is "The development of each child's capacities to the fullest."

Highly abstract values such as this one and those cited earlier can function as symbolic commitments that could inspire or motivate members of the organization and reinforce their sense of participating in worthwhile work. At the same time, the statement of abstract goals can easily become ritualistic and have little or no relationship to the day-to-day activities of the organization. The gap between ideals and behavior is a commonplace one that represents a genuine challenge to those who wish to move their organizations toward more desirable futures. Their task is to translate abstract values into specific organizational commitments and activities. This task is a complex one that should be considered in conjunction with the problem of the development of enlarged organizational capabilities for reflective valuation, a topic considered as part of our treatment of institutionalization below.

Here the emphasis is on the search for desirable futures via procedures that scan an array of values. Having discussed several ways of scanning directly for particular values, some less direct techniques should be considered. For example, one can scan for particular organizational problems. Such problems could range from student-on-student violence to low faculty morale. The relevant values could then be more directly addressed as part of an effort not only to resolve the problem at hand but also to enhance the positive values involved, in the first case, students' respect for one another. A problem of a more general kind that is quite common in organizations that have ambiguous or abstract goals is goal displacement. Goal displacement refers to situations where the means to an end becomes an end in itself. An example in schools would be when pupil control, which is a means to the end of learning, becomes an end in itself. A related kind of problem is suggested by Hemphill's distinction between attempted, successful, and effective leadership acts. The first fails in the attempt to devise a structure to deal with a problem, the second successfully puts in place a structure for problem resolution, and the third puts such a structure in place and is effective; that is, it resolves the problem.

Most organizations, especially those whose outcomes are vague, will exhibit a variety of successful, but not very effective, structures. We are all familiar with the committee that was praised for its efforts but did little to resolve the problem it was created to address. Successful but ineffective structures can sometimes contribute to the resolution of other problems than those that they were charged to solve, such as when a committee set up to deal with the problem of drug use in schools helps improve public relations while failing to influence drug use. Administrators need to be sensitive to subtle problems such as goal displacement and successful but not effective structures if they are to move their organizations forward in substantive ways.

A relatively simple way to search for desirable futures is to put in place mechanisms for various groups and individuals to suggest organizational improvements. Such mechanisms should include procedures both to elicit and to assess suggestions. The assessment could explicate values implicit in the suggestions as part of that process. Finally, in some cases, it may be possible for school organizations to "cogwheel" their needs with certain community needs. A pertinent example is to draw on capable older people, who too often live idle and lonely lives, to contribute in special ways to the instructional program. Another is the use of student volunteers in particular community activities. Cogwheeling of this kind can help to attain a variety of values. In the case of the last example, students would have opportunities to model good citizenship, probably enhance their social skills, and develop a more sensitive awareness of a particular social problem while contributing something to its resolution.[2]

Whether or not they use any of the scanning procedures we mentioned, good administrators should cultivate a vision of what their organizations, at their best, might become. The need to move toward more desirable futures will be ever present because there are no final victories in this kind of struggle. But there will be some victories along with the unavoidable defeats and, in educational organizations, even small victories are worth achieving because they usually result in better futures for particular individuals.

Alternative Solutions to Moral Problems
and Consequence Analysis

Most of the moral problems faced by administrators come up in the normal course of daily events. Many of them can be resolved quite quickly. They do not require extended analysis because the competing values in the case are clearly of unequal moral force. For instance, if parents make an outlandish demand for special treatment for their child without being able to present supporting reasons, or for reasons that clearly have nothing to do with the welfare of the child and even may be educationally unsound, the problem quickly changes. It is no longer a matter of examining the merits of the demand and the probable consequences of acceding to it or rejecting it. The problem is now how to explain to the parents the reasons why their request cannot be granted and to attempt to persuade them that such a decision is fair.

The request for special treatment going beyond that usually extended to students with special problems is a classic case in education. It pits the real or imagined good of a student against a variety of other potential values such as the equity of the request in terms of other students, the matter of perceived fairness by other students and parents, and sometimes the interests of teachers or other staff who may have some involvement. One well-known case puts that kind of issue in bold relief.[3] A boy is transferred from an older school to a newer one in the school district on the basis of a physician's letter that later appears fraudulent on quite compelling but circumstantial evidence. Some parents know about this and are asking that their children also be transferred. The school district has a history of disputes over school boundary lines, and a prospective building program could be endangered by the reopening of these disputes. The newer school is widely perceived to be better than the older one, and most parents would prefer that their children go to the newer building. The boy was unhappy and unsuccessful in the older school but has shown evidence of substantial growth at the newer school.

We present this case in simplified form to illustrate consequence analysis. It is a difficult case because of the juxtaposition of the student's positive turnaround at the new school with the apparent dishonesty involved in the transfer and its potential fallout for the district building program. There are two major alternatives. One is to keep the student where he is and the other is to retransfer him now

or at a later time. Student welfare is an obvious concern of importance. On the one hand, the transferred student is doing better in the
new school and could regress if he were returned to his former
school. On the other hand, the welfare of the students as a group
could be threatened if this incident were to become a roadblock to a
needed school building program.

Viewed in terms of probable negative consequences, the first
option has consequences that are largely educational and personal-
social for the student in question. The second option could fuel community discontent with the fairness of student assignment policies
and perhaps derail or delay improved school facilities for the district
and its students. The consequences of the first option seem more
directly predictable than those of the second. Also, the consequences
of the first option appear somewhat more manageable; that is, they
appear easier to mitigate.

It seems clear that if the retransfer option is chosen, it will be
imperative to plan and monitor the instructional program of the student. Counselors should also be involved to help the student adjust.
If the stay-in-place option is selected, written recommendations based
on educational and psychological considerations should become
part of the record to justify the decision. A key concept would be
fairness, expressed in the rationale that what was done for this student would be done for any student in the same circumstances. To
deal with an additional consequences of the staying-in-place option,
disapproval of the deception involved in the transfer would have to
be communicated unequivocally to the parents and to the student,
who apparently had boasted about it to some of his friends. Otherwise, a decision made to further an individual student's education
and growth could have a negative effect on student education within
the district.

The point of this exercise is straightforward. Either option could
be handled well or badly, depending on whether likely consequences
are considered. When the consequences of a decision are dealt with
as part of that decision, the choice is a better one because it recognizes that decisions are not isolated but occur in social contexts, often
with a variety of effects. These effects, which arise as a result of
selecting from competing moral alternatives, can themselves generate new ethical issues. Because of this problem, it is critical that at
least the more important probable consequences of alternative
courses of action be considered prior to choice and implementation.

Consequence Analysis as a Process

Consequence analysis is commonly a reflective activity. Decision makers and their colleagues try to think of and anticipate the main consequences of various alternatives. It is also a predictive activity because it is the probable or likely consequences that are the main concern. The effort to explicate consequences can also be thought of as an attempt to reduce unintended and unanticipated consequences.

There are a number of processes that can be helpful in consequence analysis. One is to use the social sciences as vehicles for general scanning. By doing so, it can be asked if there are psychological consequences for given individuals; sociological consequences in terms of groups, segments of the community, and so on; political consequences in terms of power, interest groups, conflict, and so forth; anthropological consequences, in terms of culture, symbols, shared meanings, and more; economic consequences, in terms of resource availability and allocation, and so on.

Within each area, various concepts and theories can be used in scanning for consequences. To take sociology as an example, formal and informal groups, norms, scripts, status, symbols, role expectations, socialization, and various explanations that employ these and other concepts might suggest probable consequences. Along these same lines, educational research and studies of organizational life can provide useful concepts that might be especially relevant to consequence analysis in school settings. Some relevant concepts and theories will be considered in our discussions of a case of attempted school improvement and of institutionalization.

Another kind of scan for consequences lists the various players in the cases, both individuals and groups, and asks whether particular courses of action are likely to have an effect on them. In school organizations, the students, teachers, specialists, staff workers, administrators, parents, other social service and public agency personnel, and community members are examples. These groups can themselves often be usefully subdivided, as when the community is seen to include various organizations and interest groups such as taxpayers' associations, ethnic clubs, religious groups, and others.

Such devices are helpful because they reduce the likelihood of missing significant consequences of a contemplated action. Also relevant from a values standpoint are consequences that might harm particular individuals and that could be countered without seriously eroding the broader purposes of the action. These kinds of devices also can alert administrators to ancillary aspects of the decision process. For example, a scan of players might serve as a reminder that certain individuals who probably would not be directly affected by a particular action should at least be informed prior to its implementation.

The devices used to elaborate consequences are limited only by the creativity of those who develop and use them. Scenario construction of varying degrees of detail and specificity figures in most of them. Special problems may require special procedures. For instance, when complex financing is a key issue, calculations of available resources and the effects of different expenditure options may be required. Such calculations are facilitated by computer programs that are already available or are readily devised.

Consequence analyses can have a current and ongoing empirical side. Gathering new information is sometimes crucial. For example, the availability of certain instructional materials might be determined in connection with a proposed curriculum change, or persons might be consulted who are knowledgeable about the likely reaction of a community group to a contemplated school action. A more comprehensive kind of data gathering occurs when a school change is carried out in stages with movement to a later stage contingent on success at an earlier one. Incremental approaches of this sort are fairly common. Often such changes are described as experimental, with assessment to take place at a given point followed by a decision about the project's future. Values enter the picture at various points because the desirability of probable effects can be reflectively examined.

There is little doubt that consequence analysis can help to ground choices and ensure that critical values are not violated in the process of attaining more desirable futures. However, an important caveat must be kept in mind. Like any method, reflection can have its weaknesses. One of them is overanalysis, which John Dewey called one of the vices of reflection.[4] Although one might argue that underanalysis is actually more of a problem, it needs to be recognized that overanalysis can prevent closure and paralyze action. Furthermore, overanalysis wastes time and energy, two commodities already in high demand in educational organizations.

The purpose of consequence analysis is to facilitate wise moral choice, not to mire it in interminable deliberations. The point is to get to the heart of the matter at hand. This means making explicit the key values involved and the discernible alternatives. To be sure, potential courses of action and their consequences must be reflectively searched for and examined, but this has to be done within existing temporal and organizational constraints. The scanning and analysis that is required, however, can ordinarily be done as part of administrator and organizational routines and strategies. In the end, it is simply a matter of making reasoned judgments informed by relevant concepts and generalizations, which is what thoughtful people do regularly. These topics will be explored more systematically in our treatment of internalization and institutionalization. Next, we turn to two additional cases.

Two Cases

The cases presented illustrate, in the first instance, the administrator-originated problem, and in the second instance, the kind of problem that is thrust on administrators in the ordinary course of organizational events.[5] Recall that the originated problem arises because of a perceived gap between a hoped-for state and the status quo, whereas the received problem occurs even when the administrator might wish it would go away. Both kinds of cases illustrate the centrality of values and of consequence analysis in decision making. In the originated problem, certain values (or conceptions of the desirable) are an explicit part of a particular school improvement program, while in the received problem, the relevant values have to be sorted out. The sketches of the cases are necessarily selective and abbreviated. The aim is illustration, not extended description. The concepts and analysis employed are simply those that seem most relevant to us in the circumstances of the cases.

Case 1: An Instructional Improvement

The first case deals with the implementation of an instructional improvement, a new social studies curriculum for the upper elementary grades that gave greater emphasis to contemporary problems such as the environment, poverty, conflict, violence, and societal fragmentation. The new curriculum came with new syllabi and textbooks that necessitated substantive changes in the subject matter taught and, to some extent, in the teaching methods used.

As often happens, the change had been adopted at the school district level but was to be implemented at the building level under the direction of the principal. The change was not arbitrary. It had a high degree of legitimation because it had been subjected to lengthy examination by a committee that included the principals and teachers from each building that would be involved. Furthermore, the new curriculum was endorsed by both the district's Parent-Teacher Council and a citizens' committee established several years earlier as an advisory body to the superintendent.

The stated purposes of the curriculum were cast in terms of the development of students as responsible citizens, knowledgeable about the country's problems, and ready to participate thoughtfully in the democratic process. These purposes and the values that they implied appeared to enjoy widespread support in the school and the community. The superintendent and principal of the school examined in the case both felt the new curriculum represented a vast improvement that would greatly benefit the students. The principal also saw it as a way of encouraging some faculty to be more thoughtful about their teaching. In her second year as principal, she sensed that she had not yet won the full support of the faculty, especially the upper-grade teachers directly affected by the change. She hoped that working with them on the new curriculum might help.

The principal was aware that although the teachers had not voiced formal opposition to the new program, many hoped it would be merely cosmetic and were irate about the hard-to-ignore new text and materials "imposed" on them, despite the fact that a districtwide teachers' committee was involved in their selection. The principal had been given a year to put the new curriculum in place, and to assist in the effort, some additional funds were allocated to the school.

Without going into greater detail, obviously a huge limitation in a situation alive with personal and contextual contingencies, how can reflective methods and relevant concepts and theories be of use? Bear in mind that this case is an example of one in which a moral judgment already has been made by a relatively broad spectrum of individuals and groups. The new curriculum was deemed to provide subject matter that had the potential to make the students better citizens. Desirable outcomes included not only general problem solving skills but knowledge that could help separate fact from fiction in areas from environmental pollution to the marketing of political candidates, as well as an appreciation of individuality, diversity, and the inclusiveness of the democratic process.

Although the choice to adopt the curriculum was morally informed, many affected teachers were not directly involved and some perceived hierarchical pressures, adding to the usual difficulties of implementation. Reflecting on this situation, the principal and her associates should make efforts to explain and emphasize the potential student outcomes that are the curriculum's main virtues. Being part of an effort aimed at desirable student learning and growth is motivating for most teachers. Teacher altruism and commitment are organizational resources that can benefit students, but the teachers themselves must believe in the connections between the new curriculum and ethically worthwhile student effects. The appeal to superordinate goals can be a powerful incentive for teachers, especially when the proposed changes are feasible and doable, as they appeared to be in the new curriculum.

In addition, there are the usual familiar concerns. The teachers should participate as partners in decisions that specify preparations for the change, including those features of instructional procedure and assessment that might be common across classrooms. Here, given the strong autonomy and turf norms that studies have shown are found among teachers, flexibility and leeway should be stressed. The overload that characterizes the work of teaching should also be recognized. For instance, planning meetings and other inservice activities ideally should not take place before or after school. To avoid that, some of the allocated funds could be used for substitute teachers. Similarly, care should be taken to anticipate anything in the new program that might lead to disorder or to student control problems. These recommendations stem from our knowledge of schools as organizations. Given our experience, we know that teachers typically value autonomy, time, and order and that most changes tend to erode all three.[6] To stave off negative consequences along these lines thus seems essential.

In concrete, evolving situations, moral evaluation must be ongoing. Thinking consequences through must consider actual consequences as they occur. In the present case, the planning sessions could not be held at convenient times, but the teachers did not make an issue of it. Apparently, as they became more familiar with the new curriculum, many of the teachers were convinced of its value and began to be more positive about the project. A trade-off occurred as new commitment counterbalanced overload. Had planning time been more of an issue, the principal and her associates would have considered other options, for instance, weekend meetings with extra pay.

Another issue was unexpected. The teachers in the lower grades in the building were not part of the project and were only marginally involved in planning. Initially happy not to be included, some eventually showed signs of hostility. They complained that the new curriculum got too much attention, even though it was "no big deal." Some even alleged that the students in the new program were more likely to be discipline problems, implying a cause-effect relationship. The principal and others worked to mitigate these unanticipated consequences once they were recognized.

Interestingly, that these consequences are not difficult to explain suggests they might have been anticipated. One consequence stems from teacher concerns for order and student control, the other reflects the proscription of bragging or being singled out, part of the egalitarian norms among teachers that have, for example, sustained teacher opposition over the years to merit pay. In any event, this case illustrates how knowledge about schools as organizations is critical to the attainment of moral purposes. Bare bones that it is, this case suggests the complexity and fallibility of efforts to attain morally desirable change in concrete situations and also the key place of judgments informed by theory.

Case 2: A Teacher's Health

The first case was an effort to move an organization toward new and desirable goals. The second presents a problem of competing values. A sixth-grade teacher, not quite 40 years old, with 15 years service in the district, suffered a stroke just after the close of school. She returned in the fall with a letter from her physician stating that she would be able to carry out her normal duties. The stroke left her with a noticeable but not severe speech impairment.

Early in the school year, the principal began to get complaints from parents, including several requests for transfer to another teacher. As the complaints mounted, the principal made several classroom observations. These led him to conclude that the teacher's performance was marginal. She appeared to be listless and fatigued and sometimes was hard to understand. The principal discussed the problem with the teacher who insisted she was able to do her job satisfactorily and pointedly added that she was now a member of a group devoted to advocacy for the handicapped that would help her fight any change in her status. The principal then talked with the superintendent, who urged him to gather more information and make a recommendation about how to proceed.

This case has two obvious, probably competing, goods: the welfare of the teacher and the welfare of the students. The teacher has suffered a physical setback and, despite her implied warning, probably feels unsure of herself and in need of supportive relationships at work. Such relationships might help her to do a better job, if she is able to do so. Yet the students should not have to suffer sustained inadequate teaching. Their welfare as a group, although lacking the poignancy of the travails of their teacher, is strongly legitimated by the purposes of the organization.

Before the principal goes any further, more information would be useful. For instance, additional data on teaching and on student outcomes would be helpful, as would a physical evaluation of the teacher by an independent physician. Compelling results could begin to make a case for a particular alternative. Assuming no such results, the principal should consider measures that might satisfy both goods to a degree. The main negative consequence of keeping the teacher in the classroom is a deficient program for the students. It could be mitigated by assisting the teacher in appropriate ways, for example, by assigning an aide who could reduce the physical demands on the teacher and by enhancing available teaching materials. The main negative consequences of removing the teacher are damages to her psychological well-being and her career. These could be mitigated by counseling, by a leave for therapy (if justified by a medical prognosis), or by transfer to a less demanding position, if one were available.

Again, the analysis is bare bones. As noted, moral evaluation has to be ongoing. Dealing with consequences can beget new consequences. For example, giving the teacher special help could alienate her or displease other teachers, if not handled carefully. Furthermore, suitable consultation is necessary because no one person can be sure if his or her perceptions and insights are reasonable and just.

Despite its complexity, an empirically oriented ethics has important advantages. As more data are gathered, it becomes more likely that they will lead to a morally desirable alternative. In the present case, if teaching is judged defective with compelling evidence, reasons for leaving the classroom can be given to the teacher who might concur if she had the students' interests at heart. Such evidence would also be pertinent if a legal proceeding could not be avoided. If the teaching were judged to be satisfactory with supporting evidence, the principal has information useful in his discussions with concerned parents. In addition, relevant information strengthens the likelihood that the principal's recommendations will be accepted by the superintendent, always problematic for a middle manager.

A Note on Practice

Writing about cases in administration does not adequately capture the fullness of the existential reality. Administrative practice is full of complexities, special contingencies, individual peculiarities, nuances, examples of goodness and chicanery, and many other experiences that validate the old saw about truth being stranger than fiction. As the cases just examined show, the values inherent in an effort to improve a curriculum or that pertain to a problem of diminishing teacher effectiveness are relatively easy to understand and to accept. Most educators want their students to be knowledgeable and capable problem solvers and are concerned about both teacher welfare and student learning. The difficulties begin with implementation of a desirable change or when values clash. It is at this point that alternatives and consequences should be reflectively developed and probed. Savvy administrators will be helped here by the expanded view afforded by the use of social science concepts and theories.

Of course, only a limited set of alternatives and consequences can be considered in any situation. As Simon emphasized, there are boundaries and limits to human rationality.[7] Because no one can think of everything, the utility of being able to get to the heart of the matter, to see the important aspects of a situation, becomes apparent. The keys to reflective administration, vision, and valuation lie in individual internalization and organizational institutionalization. Stated differently, the kind of moral practice we envision should become part of the way that individuals and the organizations within which they work commonly and routinely respond to the problems they face. We turn next to these topics.

Notes

1. A classic example of such writers is Willard Waller, *The Sociology of Teaching* (New York: Wiley, 1932). The notion of adventure bears some kinship to our concept of robustness and the studies done of the more robust aspects of school life. See D. J. Willower and J. W. Licata, "Environmental Robustness and School Structure," *Planning and Changing* 6 (1975): 120-27 and the review piece J. W. Licata and B. L. Johnson, "Toward a Synthesis of Inquiry on Environmental Robustness," *Planning and Changing* 20 (1989): 215-30.

2. The classic on goal displacement is R. K. Merton, *Social Theory and Social Structure* (New York: Free Press, 1968). On leadership acts, see J. K. Hemphill, "Administration as Problem-Solving," in *Administrative Theory in Education*, ed. A. W. Halpin (New York: Macmillan, 1967). On cogwheeling, see D. J. Willower, "Schools, Values and Educational Inquiry," *Educational Administration Quarterly* 9 (1973): 1-18.

3. A simplified version is given of the case, "The Letter," in C. G. Sargent and E. L. Belisle, *Educational Administration: Cases and Concepts* (Boston: Houghton Mifflin, 1955). The discussion of consequence analysis in this case is based on D. J. Willower, "The Professorship in Educational Administration: A Rationale," in *The Professorship in Educational Administration*, ed. D. J. Willower and J. A. Culbertson (Columbus, OH and University Park, PA: University Council for Educational Administration and The Pennsylvania State University, 1964).

4. J. Dewey, *Human Nature and Conduct* (New York: Henry Holt, 1922), 197-98.

5. The two cases are taken, with minor changes, from D. J. Willower, "Values, Valuation and Explanation in School Organizations," *Journal of School Leadership* 4 (1994): 466-83.

6. For elaboration, see D. J. Willower, "School Reform and Schools as Organizations," *Journal of School Leadership* 1 (1991): 305-15.

7. H. A. Simon, *Administrative Behavior* (New York: Macmillan, 1958). It should also be kept in mind that the general processes used to solve problems show striking similarities to what are variously labeled the methods of inquiry, reflective methods, or scientific methods, and to what we call valuation. For a review of that research, see R. J. Sternberg and J. E. Davidson, "Problem Solving," in *Encyclopedia of Educational Research* (6th ed., Vol. 3), ed. M. C. Alkin (New York: Macmillan, 1992).

·5·

Moral Practice
Individuals and Organizations

Individuals

As Dewey long ago pointed out, most human behavior is based on impulse and habit, but problem resolution depends on the mediation of thought and reflection.[1] Clearly, most people, most of the time, are not engaged in reflection on new purposes and goals, their desirability, and how to move toward those that hold the most promise. Given the biological and psychological makeup of human beings, Dewey understood how crucial it was for the use of reflective methods to become habitual and natural, something that individuals could do almost automatically. He also fully recognized the part played by emotion, commitment, and passion in the human condition. He saw the separation of intellect and emotion as a moral tragedy that makes scientific thinking seem cold and calculating, cutting off generous and sympathetic impulse and emotion from its best hope of clarification and realization.

The person who is able to internalize reflective methods recognizes that emotion does not always serve good purposes. For such a person, desire raises the question of desirability. Although desire is immediate and mechanical, desirability emerges from deliberation. For the individual, this can lead to an integration of desires based on their quality and longer-range considerations, resulting in fuller, richer experience and growth. In this view, character is seen as a working interaction of habits. Someone who has been able to internalize reflective methods, who has a well-developed and committed sense of human possibilities and the will to search out feasible ways that they might be achieved, would be someone of good character. Despite its moral significance and key place in defining a good human being, good character is no guarantee of good outcomes. However, it seems likely that the individual who employs reflective methods and engages in the kind of valuation we have described will avoid at least some of the negative consequences of alternative choices and may achieve some success in attaining morally desirable results.

Interestingly, recent studies using frameworks from cognitive science have shown that expert, as contrasted with novice, administrators demonstrate reflective and deliberative abilities. This line of inquiry, influenced by Herbert Simon and what has been called the Carnegie School, has been advanced most notably in educational administration by the careful work of Leithwood and his colleagues.[2] The Leithwood studies also include some research on values in administrator decision making.

Such research is in its infancy in educational administration. Definitional and operational problems include concerns about levels of abstraction, overlap versus mutual exclusivity of concepts, and the gap between verbalization and behavior that is so common in moral affairs. In terms of the perspective we advanced, the more we can know about the variables associated with reflective choice, which in the context of ethics is a blending of scientific thinking and moral commitment, the better.

Of interest, too, are concepts such as character, just discussed, that seem so central to the moral self and yet is so underresearched. Various commonly called for qualities can also be explored empirically. A case in point is the kind of self-awareness and willingness to be self-critical suggested by G. H. Mead's concept of reflexiveness. An older version, of course, is the Socratic dictum cast in the Delphic aphorism, "Know thyself." Such self-knowledge can serve as an adjunct to reflective methods because it can help an administrator correct for personal bents and biases. Along these same lines, a conscious effort to set aside presuppositions of the kind employed in phenomenological analysis can also facilitate reflective thought.[3]

The administrator who wants to employ reflective methods will have to make a conscious decision and effort to do so. Just as reflective methods require the mediation of thought, so too does the choice to use them. Genuine internalization means that eventually reflective thinking becomes a habit, a virtually automatic response to problematic situations or, in administrative terms, nonroutine decisions. There are no intrinsic reasons why thoughtful individuals cannot successfully internalize such methods, however imperfectly they may do so. Indeed, reflective decision making is arguably the mark of the good administrator and the good person.

It is important to keep in mind, however, that individuals are social creatures. Their behavior takes place in social contexts that can aid or hinder reflective approaches to problems. We turn next to the organizational context within which administration occurs.

Organizations

Various terms are used to refer to organizations that are characterized by more or less institutionalized efforts to employ reflective methods. *Educative, learning, inquiry based, problem solving* and of course, *reflective organizations* are some examples. Our guess is that the term *problem solving* would communicate the general idea more directly to more people.

This may be an appropriate point at which to reemphasize that reflective methods are for problem solving. Most human interactions and organizational activities are carried out spontaneously and easily without noticeable deliberation. That is the usual and normal situation. Reflective methods are most useful when there are problems to be dealt with, including those that may arise when alternatives to the status quo are considered. It is at such times that the quality of decisions will be influenced by whether reflective methods have been internalized at the level of the individual and institutionalized at the level of the organization.

Here, institutionalization means incorporation into the everyday life and routine of the organization, something that becomes part of the organization's social fabric and ongoing activity. Institutionalization has a cultural side that is concerned with values, norms, shared meanings, and symbols and an official side that is concerned with more formal practices, events, and procedures.

An organization that employs reflective methods must be open to all kinds of ideas yet devoted to their critical assessment as well. The following kinds of comments might be heard in such an organization: "We're always looking for good ideas." "We try to figure out ahead of time if something will work." "We check things out and debug them." "We're not afraid to criticize ideas." "We look at all sides of a problem, then try to do the right thing." If the values and attitudes suggested by such comments are to flourish in an organization, it seems essential that they have the support of the formal leadership and most participants.

The use of reflective methods in organizations has many advantages. The exploration of consequences helps to ensure that there will be fewer failures. The airing of pros and cons makes decisions relatively easy to defend because most objections have already been explored and the decision has survived critical analysis. Reflective methods also direct attention toward reasons and away from the defensiveness, feigned deference, and game playing that is so often spawned by considerations of hierarchy. In the same vein, when a decision goes wrong, the focus is on why rather than on who is to blame. The use of reflective methods also seems particularly fitting in school organizations that have learning and education as their main purposes.

Moving Toward Reflective Problem Solving

The advantage of reflective methods, some of which were just noted, provide powerful reasons for their widespread use in organizations, as well as in everyday life. However, moving toward a situation where they become a natural, customary response to problems is itself problematic. Some of the common ills of organizational life, especially those stemming from such sources as needs for status, single-minded adherence to a particular set of pregiven beliefs, identification with a special interest group, and commitment to familiar but ineffective practices, are obvious barriers to the implementation of reflective methods.

Such barriers can be mitigated by simple procedures that subject proposed courses of action to critical analysis. A regular part of the decision process in the various organizational councils, committees, and other forums where decisions are formulated should be "what can go wrong" sessions, pro and con explorations, consequence analysis, or other similar procedures. What they are called is less important than ensuring that they become routinized and accepted as integral to organizational choice. Roles that aid processes such as that of a devil's advocate can also be helpful.

An important concern in any effort to move toward reflective decision making is the legitimation of criticism. Criticism ordinarily is not very welcome. It can threaten beliefs and ideas and by extension, their holders, by subjecting them to public scrutiny and perhaps rejection or revision. Commonly, personal interactions are buffered by informal, but shared, understandings. For instance, disagreeable opinions and foolish ideas are often politely ignored and not called into question. Such behavior helps to maintain positive relationships in social settings. This suggests that the use of reflective methods and especially critical analysis in organizations should attend to the comfort level of participants and make civility, good manners, and respect for individuals part of the decision making environment. Criticism should be depersonal in the sense that it is directed to ideas, not to their originator or proponents. In this process, administrators can lead by example by subjecting their own ideas to criticism and encouraging others to do the same.

Whatever processes and procedures are used, it is essential that the members of the organization understand that reflective methods are employed to facilitate wise decision making that furthers the attainment of desirable outcomes. This commitment to school improvement through the use of reflective methods is one that can provide common ground and direction to the organization and those who participate in it. As reflective methods become more familiar and routine, the kinds of comments described earlier about how things are done in the organization should become more common, and stories about how particular pitfalls were avoided and problems resolved will become part of the school's lore.

Ordinarily, people want to be part of something worthwhile that goes beyond mere personal gain and self-promotion. Educators, in particular, often cite the desire to help others as a reason for their career choice. Reflective methods should have strong connections to good purposes and shared values. Because such methods can help both the selection of meaningful problems and the implementation of solutions, those connections are not difficult to make.

Some Organizational Features of Schools

For most organizations, the institutionalization of reflective methods represents an innovation. Clearly, innovations are nurtured by success. Success comes from choosing problems that can be solved, but success also comes by awareness of the character of the organizational and community setting in question. Although every organization and community has its own special history and peculiarities, the typical American public school exhibits a number of characteristics that are relevant to any effort to enhance reflective processes and move toward improved futures.[4]

Among the most salient characteristics are political vulnerability, student clients who may or may not have a favorable view of the school's services and their participation, high population and activity densities (a lot of people and things going on in a relatively small area), and teaching employees who are college trained and state certified. These characteristics have important consequences for the organization. The school's political vulnerability, legitimated by its status as a public agency in a democratic society, can result in pressures from individuals such as parents and a variety of special interest groups who may wish the organization to respond to their particular needs and concerns. The problematic motivation of students, along with the school's high population and activity densities, spawn a high level of routinization and a substantial number of regulations and controls directed mainly toward the pupils. The training level of the teachers, who dispense the organization's core service, leads to strong norms for autonomy in this group. Because there is no widely accepted work technology, that is, no single right way to teach and because teaching occurs in the isolation of the classroom, those norms are often accepted in the organization, as long as there are no apparent difficulties. In addition, because of the uncertain cooperation of students, especially in the large group setting of the classroom and the wide range of curricular activities, teachers' work (like that of administrators) features numerous interactions, interruptions, and a general overload. As a result, teachers place high value on order, student discipline, and time, a commodity they see as in short supply.

This kind of analysis is, of course, very useful from a theoretical, that is to say explanatory, point of view. To take one example, changes in education easily can run afoul of opposition and rejection (or acceptance that is merely ritualistic) because allowances were not made for the conditions just discussed. Most changes have the potential to violate the very things teachers prize most—autonomy, order, and time. Changes ordinarily require teachers to do something different, thus delimiting their autonomy. Changes usually make demands for extra time and effort as new ways are learned and incorporated into ongoing activities, and finally, changes typically disturb current routines and sometimes feature inherently less orderly, more individualized activities for students.

Some Implications

These considerations help to explain why school organizations are slow to change. Internally, most changes intrude on teachers' work lives in ways that discomfort them. Externally, changes may be opposed by community members or groups who may not approve of them. These realities stack the deck against successful changes because teachers' active participation and commitment ordinarily are essential to school improvement, as is community support or at least acceptance.

Our purpose in looking at schools in this way is not so much to provide a discussion of change in itself but to call attention to some considerations that are relevant to the problem of institutionalizing reflective problem solving. The broad implications of our analysis are obvious. They tell us to be sensitive to potential teacher concerns over issues related to autonomy, time, and order.

Using reflective problem solving methods clearly will require time. Deliberation, looking at alternatives and their likely consequences, and coming to an agreed-on course of action cannot be instantly accomplished. The trick here is to establish arrangements and routines that facilitate such decision making. Administrators have more flexible schedules than teachers and can usually make time for these activities, despite the fact that many do not do so in a systematic way. Although current decision forums can be readily reworked to incorporate reflective processes, and it makes sense to start there, the broader question of teacher time allocation should be addressed.

The teacher overload problem (too much to do in too little time) is well documented. It stems, in large part, from the one-to-many relationship of teachers to students and the diversity of students as persons. Moreover, most teachers deal with relatively large numbers of students throughout most of the day, facing either successions of changing cohort groups or, at the elementary school level, one or two groups for a longer period of time. When they are not working directly with their students, they are usually reading and assessing student work or preparing teaching materials.[5]

The development of new technologies, in our judgment, presents genuine opportunities for a better allocation of teacher time than is commonly found today in schools. Currently available resources such as large group instruction via films and videotapes, small group or individual instruction using computers, peer tutoring, and community volunteers all can be employed in a variety of systematic configurations to restructure the teaching day so that teachers can spend more time in planning and decision making.

Such arrangements also could counter losses of individual teacher autonomy with the gained opportunities for teachers to influence school policies and practices. Reflective problem solving ordinarily can be a threat to teacher autonomy because it might call into question some favored methods or solutions. It could become a broader threat if, as a result of reflective analysis, major curriculum and instructional changes were made that affected each classroom. The same is true with regard to order: Favored styles of discipline might not fare well under critical examination and major changes in teaching procedures and curricular subject matter and organization could create pupil control problems.

At the same time, it should be kept in mind that an important feature of the use of reflective methods is the recognition that applications and solutions must take into account the particular circumstances of a given situation. Teacher judgments at this level are encouraged and expected in an organization that has incorporated the use of reflective methods, with it being understood that there should be good reasons for the judgments made. A key consideration is the possibility that efforts to move a school organization toward more reflective problem solving, as well as toward particular courses of action proposed as a result of using such problem solving methods, will be *perceived* as threats to teacher welfare and well-being. Such perceptions can become significant barriers to school improvement for, as W. I. Thomas's famous dictum reminds us, if situations are defined as real, they are real in their consequences. Fed by endless successions of mindless fads and quick fixes, teacher suspicion of new proposals and projects is readily understood and deserving of considerable sympathy.

An important difference between reflective problem solving and most other proposals for improvement is that the former has no body of dogma to prescribe. It is simply the use of methods that are based on the best procedures and information available to solve problems and move toward better futures. Such methods appeal to common sense because they examine consequences and seek results rather than ask for commitments to pregiven solutions. So, once understood, reflective methods can be liberating and empowering, and although our focus is organizational, they can be used in other settings to deal with the problems and moral choices faced in everyday life.

Within the organization, they also have the various advantages discussed earlier. In addition, once the shared meanings and values associated with reflective problem solving become part of the organizational culture, a heightened sense of community can develop as these methods are routinely used to further desirable outcomes. Such an organizational culture, by the nature of its shared meanings and values, challenges the homogenizing, darker side of culture, which, in a word, is conformity. An organizational culture grounded in reflective problem solving is essentially an educative culture, not an oppressive one. Open to alternative ideas and values but committed to their critical assessment, this kind of culture is particularly fitting for educational organizations.[6]

Returning to the school's organizational characteristics and their implications for desirable change, it is important to recognize that, although the deck is stacked against most efforts to improve, the situation is far from hopeless. For example, even though autonomy, command of time, and order are important to teachers, these concerns do not by themselves determine teacher behavior. People in general, and educators in particular, want to contribute to something worthwhile that can be valued in itself rather than as an instrument of personal gain. Stated differently, altruism and commitments to ethically justified purposes can override the usual barriers to school improvement.

Nevertheless, administrators should take organizational arrangements and the common concerns of teachers very seriously. Altruism needs reinforcement, nurturing, and organizational routines that ease its path, or it will wither. Furthermore, a large element of realism needs to be part of faculty idealism. Everyone should understand that not every proposed improvement will succeed and that well-intended efforts will sometimes lead to unexpected and undesirable outcomes. Although such possibilities are often uncovered and presumably headed off when consequences analysis is employed as part of reflective problem solving procedures, there will always be some miscalculations or omissions.

This discussion regarding teachers can be used to model approaches with other relevant school groups. For example, community members and groups also have particular concerns and interests. They also can be appealed to in terms of larger purposes, ordinarily the good of the children and youth of the community. Furthermore, public forums for the discussion of educational issues can themselves be cast in terms of reflective problem solving methods. Proposals for desirable change that emerge after the application of such methods probably will be shorn of their less defensible features and more likely to gain wide approval. Still, there will be times when irreconcilable interests will clash and conflict will occur. At this point, reflective methods remain crucial but become more oriented to the examination of alternative political strategies in the larger context of the values being sought.

Reflective Methods and Concrete Problems

We want to reemphasize that reflective methods are genuinely useful in resolving problems, devising desirable futures and ways of attaining them, and generally in promoting thoughtful and wise decision making. Furthermore, such methods engage and challenge and are capable of eliciting excitement, passion, and emotional commitment. Reflective problem solving methods are not arcane or difficult. For instance, the search for desirable futures can be seen simply as "How can we improve things around here?" and consequence analysis as "What's liable to happen if we do it this way?"

At the same time, such methods can draw on the best thinking and analysis available to the organization and represent engaged intelligence in action. Problem solving methods are all the more important in an era of unreason where single issue advocates, demands for immediate gratification, and self-centered ideologies combine with mass media that feature brief sound bites and, far too often, sensationalism and crass materialism.

Valuation of the kind we propose weds values and knowledge to real situations. The human drama is, after all, played out in concrete activities and, in modern society, often in organizations. Valuation sets an agenda for the caring, thoughtful administrator and those with whom he or she works. We turn next to the vignettes, cases, and other exercises that illustrate and help to give reality to reflective problem solving in practice.

Notes

1. This section draws on D. J. Willower, "Dewey's Theory of Inquiry and Reflective Administration," *Journal of Educational Administration* 32 (1994): 5-22 and from the same author's *Educational Administration: Inquiry, Values, Practice* (Lancaster, PA and Basel, Switzerland: Technomic, 1994). Dewey's thinking on this topic is presented in his *Human Nature and Conduct* (New York: Henry Holt, 1922). Dewey's *The Quest for Certainty* (New York: Minton, Balch, 1929) is also a good source.

2. See K. Leithwood and R. Steinbach, *Expert Problem Solving* (Albany: SUNY Press, 1995). An earlier study that came to a similar conclusion is J. K. Hemphill, D. E. Griffiths, and N. Fredericksen, *Administrative Performance and Personality* (New York: Teachers College Press, 1962). On the influence of the Carnegie School, see P. J. DiMaggio and W. W. Powell, "Introduction," in *The New Institutionalism in Organizational Analysis*, ed. W. W. Powell and P. J. DiMaggio (Chicago: Chicago University Press, 1991).

3. These days, the term *phenomenology* often is used promiscuously in education and social science writing. We use it here to refer to the philosophy and especially to the phenomenological method set forth by E. Husserl. See his *Ideas: General Introduction to Pure Phenomenology*, trans. W. R. B. Gibson (New York: Macmillan, 1931). See also M. Farber, *The Foundation of Phenomenology* (Cambridge, MA: Harvard University Press, 1943); M. Farber, *Naturalism and Subjectivism* (Springfield, IL: Charles C Thomas, 1959).

4. See D. J. Willower, "School Reform and Schools as Organizations," *Journal of School Leadership* 1 (1991): 305-15.

5. See L. C. McDaniel-Hine and D. J. Willower, "Elementary School Teachers' Work Behavior," *Journal of Educational Research* 81 (1988): 274-80, and sources cited therein.

6. Organizational culture is usually defined as the shared meanings, values, norms, and symbols found in a given organization. Sometimes it is rendered more simply as "the way we do things around here." A well-known work on organizational culture is T. E. Deal and A. A. Kennedy, *Organizational Culture* (Reading, MA: Addison-Wesley, 1982). A more recent work is E. H. Schein, *Organizational Culture and Leadership*, 2d ed. (San Francisco: Jossey-Bass, 1992). On school cultures see D. J. Willower, "Waller and Schools as Organizations," in *Willard Waller on Education and Schools*, ed. D. J. Willower and W. L. Boyd (Berkeley, CA: McCutchan, 1989).

· 6 ·

Teaching Consequence Analysis

The Case Method

The preceding chapters have focused on the presentation of a philosophical approach to values in administration that emphasizes valuation. The use of valuation in ethical decision making to select a course of action that seems likely to attain valued outcomes requires consequence analysis. The process of teaching and learning consequence analysis cannot be merely an abstract exercise but instead must be an exercise that focuses on a nonroutine set of problematic circumstances that might be referred to as a dilemma of practice. We have already presented examples of such dilemmas: the possible transfer of a student from school A to school B, potential teacher resistance to a curriculum change, and the disabled teacher who persists even at the risk of her students' progress. Each dilemma challenges the administrator to make a wise choice from a number of alternative courses of action. Because a dilemma of practice constitutes the stimulus for teaching and learning consequence analysis, our experience suggests that the case method is a particularly appropriate teaching strategy.

The case method has a long tradition in the teaching of administration with many variations ranging from a professor leading the discussion of a written text of the case with students, to simulation and role playing to individual student use of interactive case simulations on CD ROM.[1] Cases provide students with problems that are very similar to the ones that they face in their actual work environments. Often missing, regardless of the case method variation employed with students, is a shared semantic and cognitive framework to guide their analysis of the problem or dilemma. We believe that consequence analysis provides such a framework. Over three decades of teaching educational administration classes and delivering the process through two statewide networks to assist beginning and veteran school administrators suggest that this process is easily adapted and applied to not only the nonroutine administrative experiences that we emphasize but also their routine ways of operating in schools.[2] Below we present some insights gained from working with the process and with many prospective and practicing school administrators.

Mentoring, Consulting, or Coaching as Teaching

We lecture when needed, but we usually teach through the cases themselves. Knowledge about subject matter and insights about process emerge naturally and we facilitate as a consultant, mentor, or coach. Each role has subtle differences in meaning but together provide an array of useful approaches to promote thoughtful practice. A major aim is to capitalize on teachable moments that arise naturally from the student's analysis of a case, student curiosity, and reflection. Cases are reproduced and copies are provided to each student. Sometimes we invent our own cases, at times seeding them with helpful concepts from the social sciences or some aspects of consequence analysis to facilitate practice. We have even experimented with student groups producing video cases based loosely on their own experiences. Sometimes, with groups of administrators, each from a different school district, actual cases in progress are shared and analyzed.

As noted, it is not unusual to begin a class or make a transition in content by handing out a case and putting students to work in small groups. The purpose is to encourage students to develop a solid grasp of the key content and process issues stemming from the case. This is done through careful coaching or questioning of student work. The instructor's questioning typically tries to provoke reflection and thoughtfulness on the part of the student. Occasionally, there is a didactic side to instructor responses, particularly when students need help in applying the consequence analysis process or when they become bogged down in overanalysis.

Introducing Consequence Analysis

We try to begin classes with the presentation of important ideas central to the process of consequence analysis itself or with concepts and frameworks from the social sciences that students might find helpful in understanding and analyzing the cases that we have them address. We do this in a number of ways. We often have them move into small groups and, without much ado, begin working on a particularly interesting or compelling case. Sometimes, we might use novelty or a touch of humor to introduce a key concept. For example, the following handout might be a vehicle to begin discussion about the importance of scanning for the consequences of proposed problem solutions.[3]

American agriculture has discovered that raising buffalo can be a profitable venture. These formerly wild animals require less supervision than domestic cattle and eat whatever grows wild in the pasture. Buffalo meat is low in fat and sells for much more per pound than beef. The only drawback is their intense herd instinct. If frightened, the leader of the herd will take off in almost any direction, with the herd following closely behind.

The American Plains Indians knew this and had a clever hunting strategy for buffalo. The hunters followed the herd and, at the appropriate moment, made enough noise to stampede the herd. The hunters timed their noise with the herd's proximity to a cliff. The buffalo followed their leader over the cliff and the hunters had groceries for the winter without firing a single arrow.

The hunters knew that lead buffalo do not engage in cooperatively defining problems with others in the herd. They understood that lead buffalo instinctively tend to chose the first alternative for action that comes to mind and rarely consider the consequences of the alternative they select. Instincts that cause buffalo to congregate in a herd for mutual protection and to flee from danger serve the buffalo well against most predators save those with superior predictive powers.

A brief introduction prepares the class for the following key points. Consider multiple courses of action (alternatives) and their consequences (including both intended and negative consequences). Predicting or anticipating consequences involves scanning the environment for the consequences associated with each alternative, enhancing intended consequences and reducing or eliminating negative consequences. Of course, we call the process for doing this consequence analysis. The best alternative is the one that exhibits the most desirable intended consequences and whose negative consequences are most easily reduced or eliminated. To apply these ideas, we follow with a case.

The new dean of a college of arts and sciences is appointed at a regional university. There are eight academic departments in the college, each with a department head who has been in that role for a number of years. Each department receives its budget funds from the general budget of the college. Although 80 percent of a department's budget is spent on salaries and fringe benefits (relatively fixed costs that vary only with vacancies and new positions for program growth), approximately 12 percent is spent on supplies and operating expenses (S&O), with the remainder spent on equipment and travel. By university contract, the rental of telephones and basic services is approximately $11,000 per department, due at the beginning of the fall semester. Long distance telephone and copying expenses account for most of the S&O spending in each department. In some departments faculty pay for much of their copying and many of their long distance calls out of their own pockets. These faculty are unhappy about their circumstances.

Over the years, due to budget constraints, the previous dean decided to give little or nothing in S&O monies to departments that had outside projects. These outside projects usually produce funds to supplement a department's normal budget. Half of the departments (whose faculties typically focus entirely on teaching classes) have nearly all S&O funds in the college. The four remaining departments make do on external monies that they generate. When external funding was lost, the previous dean did not make appropriate adjustments in S&O funding because he "did not want to reward departments for losing external funding and undermine departments with a tradition of excellence in teaching."

After many years, the distribution of outside projects had changed quite a bit but the allocations of college S&O funds had not. The new dean has decided to realign S&O allocations to departments based on present needs and common sense. Below is a list of departments and their S&O funding before the new dean's attempt to change the allocations.

TABLE 6.1

Department	Number of Faculty	Internal S&O	External S&O
A	12	$ 8,765	$ 2,302
B	15	$11,097	$12,118
C	11	$ 5,432	$ 5,234
D	17	$ 9,125	$ 1,008
E	15	$ 6,176	$ 2,765
F	13	$18,231	$ 4,876
G	14	$21,987	$ 7,600
H	19	$ 1,396	$33,112

The dean needs the support of the department heads and faculty to address other matters that the college will face in the future. If the dean handles implementation of the decision to redistribute funds poorly, neither faculty nor department heads will be pleased by the outcome.

Although this case comes from a higher education context, this could have been written about the budgeting of departments in a comprehensive high school or a vocational school. In addition to school administration cases, we sometimes vary the context to suggest the possible use of consequence analysis to other administrative positions and other aspects of life. In this case, rather than dealing with generating and selecting from among different solutions, our aim is to follow the introduction of consequence analysis with an initial experience that places the focus on consequences rather than on alternatives. We suggest that the dean probably had a number of possible alternatives available. Before we get into the process of choosing from among multiple alternatives, however, we ask our students to focus on the decision the dean has already made (redis-tribute S&O funds).

Our purpose is to help students become initially familiar with con-sequence identification and implementation. We ask them to (a) state the probable intended consequences of this decision, (b) identify the negative consequences of the decision, and (c) explain how they might mitigate or eliminate these negatives. We follow their analysis with a discussion. At this point, students usually begin to express interest in generating other alternatives and some systematic ways of scanning for consequences, particularly negative consequences.

Working Through the Process

Generating Alternatives

Let us consider two methods that we use to help students generate alternative solutions to a dilemma of practice: the critical approach and the noncritical approach.[4] Because most students usually turn to the critical approach without thinking about other ways of generating alternatives, little instruction or encouragement from the instructor seems necessary. This approach occurs when an individual, or a group of individuals, generates one possible alternative at a time and criticize it immediately. This approach has been shown to be effective in producing a small number of high quality alternatives in a relatively short period of time.[5] The critical approach is especially well suited to problem situations that are considered urgent and may not require highly creative solutions. An example might be when a superinten-dent asks a school principal for recommendations on how she would cut her school budget by 10 percent and requests an answer by the next day.

The noncritical approach, popularly known as "brainstorming," has been shown to be effective in producing a large number of alter-natives.[6] This method of generating alternatives is probably best employed in situations where a large number of creative alternatives are needed for consideration and where urgency is not a problem. Brainstorming is based on the rationale that people tend to be more creative and reflective when they know that their ideas will not receive immediate criticism.[7] For instance, a newly consolidated school district combines two smaller ones: one composed of mostly American Indian students and one composed of mostly Anglo and Hispanic students. A committee of concerned citizens and educators, charged with developing a vision for their new school district, probably have the time to employ a brainstorming strategy. Such a strategy provides an opportunity for all points of view to be heard without immediate evaluation and may produce a relatively creative and thoughtful response to their charge. When our students are asked to do consequence analysis in groups, we specifically ask them to choose between the critical and noncritical methods based on the needs of the case. The instructor can influence the degree of urgency by specifying the time for the completion of the analysis.

Intended Consequences

Alternatives aimed at solving dilemmas of practice can be opportunities for administrators or problem-solving groups to make clear their intentions and expectations. The accomplishment of one or more intended consequences is a key aspect of any course of action directed at a nonroutine problem. From this point of view, alternatives are seen as possible ways to bring about preferred outcomes consistent with the community's desired future for the school. For example, a group of our students once analyzed a case in which a number of nonroutine problems faced by a particular high school principal seemed rooted in widespread community apathy about school programs and student progress. After going through a brief brainstorming exercise, they identified a number of promising alternatives. One student approach was to decentralize community involvement opportunities. The rationale was that community involvement would be more likely if it addressed local needs. They proposed five separate PTA locals, each part of a larger PTA network. The intended consequence was increased community support from faculty and parents. A second dimension to the decentralization plan called for inviting each business or public agency in the community to adopt a homeroom. The intended consequence here was increased support from the business and professional community.

Scanning for Negative Consequences

As we have already seen, consequence analysis can encourage thoughtful and ethical practice. It is a reflective activity involving the

selection of alternatives for testing, the prediction of likely consequences, and efforts to reduce anticipated and unanticipated negative
consequences. Recall that one of the scanning frameworks that we have
already introduced is the social sciences, scanning for psychological,
sociological, political, anthropological, or economic consequences.
We suggested that various concepts and theories from these areas can
be used in scanning for consequences. Examples ranged from formal
and informal groups to role expectations, socialization, and various
theoretical explanations. Although these can be presented in a lecture
format or reading assignments, their relevance is clearer when they
are introduced in connection with a case that might best employ one
or more of these concepts and theories.

   Let's consider a scanning framework that we might recommend to
students analyzing a case dealing with an associate superintendent's
or a school principal's attempt to implement or modify a program or
policy. This scanning framework integrates material from sociology
and psychology as well as from research on schools as organizations.
In part, the framework focuses on the norms present in the teacher
subculture emphasizing the need for autonomy in classroom decision making and pupil control. Teachers experience ample psychological stress from the "stimulus overload" environment in which
they work. The political and public vulnerability of the school
organization is still another consideration.[8] Although they understand that there may be other important aspects to consider, four
questions serve as initial guides for anticipating probable teacher
and community reactions to the proposed program or policy change:

1. Will implementation of this alternative threaten teachers'
   sense of autonomy?
2. Will implementation of this alternative threaten teachers'
   confidence about their ability to maintain adequate pupil
   control?
3. Will implementation of this alternative increase the hin-
   drance level (extra paper work, extra meetings and duties)
   to teaching?
4. Will the responses of various community groups or agencies
   to this alternative increase teachers' sense of public vulnerability?

If the answer to any of these questions suggests teacher or community resistance to program implementation, administration students are likely to consider this a negative consequence of the proposed program or policy and think about possible modifications that would reduce or eliminate the anticipated negative consequences exposed through scanning. This framework is a favorite of administration students because of the importance of teacher groups in implementing decisions, policies, and innovation.

Below are vignettes that we sometimes use to give students practice with the questions listed above as scanning devices. We ask students to anticipate the negative consequences of each of these four cases:

1. The legislature passes a bill requiring teachers to visit the home/parents of students who have failed their class during a particular quarter. Teachers and parents are to design individualized plans to improve student progress.

2. A particular school board has required each school to establish an advisory council composed of three students, three teachers, three parents, and one member of the business community. All members are to be elected by those they represent. The principal serves ex-officio. This council makes policy that the professional staff must implement. The council at the high school in this district has decided to recognize excellence in teaching as its first initiative.

3. A local company has donated a computer and software for each classroom in a large elementary school. In exchange, the principal has promised that each teacher would employ the computer in delivering instruction. The principal has not consulted his teachers because he wants the delivery of the computers to be a pleasant surprise, one that might improve student and teacher morale.

4. During the last assembly of the school year, a group of seniors toss blue and white paint (school colors) from the balcony as a prank. Teacher and student clothing are ruined and cleanup costs are high. Faculty are quite upset about this incident. The principal recommends to the superintendent that these students not be allowed to participate in graduation exercises. The superintendent does not want to ruin graduation for the parents of these students. He directs the students to clean up the mess. Parents agree to pay the damages.

Sometimes this scanning framework may not produce enough systematic scanning to predict the widest array of possible negative consequences needed for successful analysis. We might suggest supplementing the first scanning process by considering a list of the various roles and social positions that are present in the school or school district. We encourage students to ask whether the particular courses of action that they are thinking about would have consequences for each role or social position. Students, teachers, specialists, staff workers, administrators, parents, other social service and public agency personnel, and community members are examples. Another, but similar, way of doing this is to scan across key groups that might include various organizations and interest groups such as taxpayers' associations, ethnic clubs, religious groups, and others. We can recall a school superintendent who kept a list of significant school groups (students, parents, school board members, central office employees, principals, teachers, support staff) under the glass top on his desk. He claimed that he scanned these groups prior to making an important decision or taking a policy position. He would reflect and ask himself about the possible positive and negative consequences of the decision for each group.

Using Consequence Analysis in the Classroom

On Teaching and Learning

The purposes of sharing the following interaction involving students and their instructor are twofold: to describe how a typical educational administration class and instructor might use consequence analysis and to give the reader additional practice with the process. The scenario depicts a typical group of administration students as they draw on selected concepts from the social sciences and implement consequence analysis. This example is presented for descriptive purposes and not necessarily as an example of the best possible response to the case. A different class working through this case may select different alternatives and focus on different sets of consequences.

The case below is one that we might use to introduce social science insights about triad interaction (interaction among three parties) and to enhance students' abilities to recognize problems at different levels of abstraction (the distinction between symptoms and problems).[9]

With that in mind, consider a classroom with educational administration students, arranged in small groups, preparing to analyze the
following case.

Don Miller is superintendent of schools in Fairfax County. He
thinks of himself as a mentor for a number of young people who
aspire to administrative posts in the district. Mary First is one of those
people. She has been appointed to the position of Assistant Principal
at Elmore High School. Because Mary has only 3 years of teaching
experience and no administrative experience, the appointment was
a bit of a surprise to many in the district. Most knew that Don Miller
and Ben First, Mary's husband, are close friends. Some suspect that
this relationship had an influence on Mary's appointment.

During the first 6 months of the school year, Mary took on more
responsibility than might have been expected of a new assistant
principal and only occasionally sought the approval of Joan Green,
the high school principal. Examples of Mary's initiatives included
implementation of an in-school suspension program and the sub-
mission of a proposal for funding a whole-language program. When
Joan asked Mary why she was not consulted in advance on some of
these matters, Mary explained that there was no problem because
she had personally discussed these ideas with Don Miller. Joan pressed
Mary each time to consult with her prior to going to the superintendent with an idea. Mary's reply was that these things just come up at
the country club and other social gatherings with the Millers, and
that it is hard to limit such conversations.

As a result of Mary's initiatives, some teachers began to question
who was running the school. Some of the English teachers were quite
upset by the decision to propose a whole-language approach without consulting them. On the other hand, the in-school suspension
program was working quite well. Unfortunately, an article in the
newspaper about a new program featured interviews with Don
Miller and Mary First without mentioning the two teachers who had
brought the innovative idea to Mary in the first place. Joan was not
mentioned in the feature.

Joan's attempts to discuss this situation with Don Miller ended
in strong praise for Mary from Miller and an emphasis on the need
to give Mary opportunities to try new things. On a number of occasions, Don Miller called the school to talk with Mary. When Joan
answered, Don would exchange small talk and then ask to talk with

Mary. Mary and Don often spent as much as a half an hour on the phone together.

Each week a number of principals meet for an informal lunch. At the most recent luncheon, Joan walked in late and was embarrassed to overhear the following conversation. One principal asked, "Do you think Joan realizes that her new 'golden girl' is undermining her authority as principal?" Another noted that some think the superintendent is running the school through Mary. Another mentioned that Don Miller had asked him, "What is wrong at Elmore? Why can't Joan make a decision?" Another principal commented that this arrangement was causing him to question his own support from the central office, "What is happening to the legitimate chain of command in this school district?" Still another whispered, "Is this a case of our superintendent's mentoring gone awry . . . or is there something going on between Don and Mary?" A younger member of the group jumped to Don's aid saying, "No, no, Don's just into this mentor thing. He has been a big help with my career. I think he just doesn't understand the harm he is doing to Joan and Mary. I think his intentions are good, but his technique is poor on this one."

Joan turned to leave, only to find herself looking into the eyes of Don Miller who had apparently overheard much of the same conversation. He whispered to her, "Joan, I had no idea. I'm sorry . . ." Embarrassed and saddened by the conversation that she overheard, Joan shook her head in acceptance of the apology and awkwardly noted her departure saying, "I have a meeting with Mary and some teachers on the whole-language proposal. I won't have time for lunch after all."

As our various student groups begin discussing these circumstances and begin recalling applicable concepts from their reading assignments, the following insights emerge. Although the organizational table for Fairfax County School District probably shows the position of assistant principal reporting to the principal, the table also requires each principal to report to an associate superintendent or to the superintendent. Informally, an alliance has developed between Mary, a new assistant principal, and Don Miller, the superintendent. Joan, the principal in Mary's school, is placed at a disadvantage by this relationship. In a sense, the relationship between Don and Mary can be thought of as improper or illegitimate in terms of formal stratification of roles.[10] Apparently, this arrangement is causing confusion and disruption in the chain of command. Joan feels a loss of power, teachers don't know who is in charge, and some principals are tempted to speculate about the integrity, competence, and trustworthiness of the superintendent.

Some administration students claim that this dilemma is common in many organizational settings, most occurring unintentionally, as appears to be the case in this vignette. One of the students in a particular group speaks out to the entire class, "I have to say that this case just raises the hair on the back of my neck. This has happened to me on more than one occasion when I worked in industry." Another agrees, "The same thing has happened to me as a nursing supervisor in a hospital." A number of others nod their heads in agreement. The instructor notes that, "A breakdown in the legitimate ordering of roles and relationships can result in negative emotions not unlike those you are recalling right now—anger, fear, outrage or a sense of abandonment." Another student follows this by suggesting that Don, Joan, and Mary all suffer in this scenario. Another speculates aloud that other principals probably worry that the same thing might happen to them someday, "Few of them would look forward to working with Mary in the future. Trusting Don's judgment about these things in the future would be unlikely." Another student notes that at the school level, some teachers are also upset by the lack of clarity about who is really in charge (Joan, Mary, or perhaps, Don Miller). Still, another student adds in a low voice, ". . . and Joan may leave the district."

The instructor moves them back to the various group discussions by saying, "You seem to not only understand this case in a reasoned and thoughtful way, but you seem to empathize with concerns of the characters. Let's continue with consequence analysis and see what we can learn from this situation." As the instructor moves unobtrusively among the groups he overhears the following. In one group, students notice that almost all of the people involved seem to hold Don Miller responsible for the confusion. They speculate that many boundary disputes and confusion over roles and responsibilities occur in the presence of good intentions gone awry, unintentional managerial error, or indecision. They can understand why the principals and others hold Don responsible for the confusion. As is the case with this student group, the rest of the class soon agrees that this is predominantly Don's problem to solve.

Another group of students decide that Don's statement of the problem should be, "What can be done to enhance the induction of new administrators in a way that is consistent with the legitimate chain of command?" They suggest that Don should work with Joan and Mary to clarify roles and responsibilities as soon as possible. Don's subsequent formal and informal communications with either would need to be consistent with the agreement on roles, responsibilities, and the appropriate chain of command. After all, the students thought, Don has the authority and responsibility to do so.[11]

One student in a particularly active group states that "Don might take the opportunity to suggest that at this point in Mary's development, Joan would be an important mentor for Mary. He might suggest that Joan, and some of the other experienced principals, would provide her with a helpful professional development network." Another student asks the instructor whether this course of action might result in Mary feeling as if she is losing a mentor. The instructor reflects a minute, then responds, "Don might note that he is pleased to be a part of her informal network but that these new arrangements expand her professional development network in ways that make everyone involved as comfortable with the process as possible." Some students are attracted to this approach, one or two remain thoughtful, then discussion resumes.

Although almost all groups come to similar conclusions, they are careful not to stop their work. They predict that if Don's mentoring continues as an out-of-pocket, ad hoc avocation of the superintendent, confusion might recur with new actors. They feel that Don has a responsibility to solve not only the symptoms of the problem (such as Joan and Mary's confusion over roles and responsibilities) but also to put in place structure (an improved induction process for new administrators) so that the symptoms would not recur. They suspect that most people in the school district value such a process for teachers and administrators.

Our students see this dilemma as an opportunity for Don to advance his personal commitment to values such as growth and leadership. These values are probably the basis of his interest in mentoring new administrators in the first place. Perhaps, work on this professional development issue could be informed by a larger vision for the entire school district that would be shared by school district personnel, students, and community members alike.

The student groups spend relatively little time on correcting the confusion about roles and responsibilities. As one of them notes, "This is a rather straightforward and routine decision. Making sure this kind of thing doesn't happen again and the improvement of administrator induction into the system, seem to be the challenges that Don must face." The students spend most of their time employing consequence analysis with the problem of how Don might develop an improved system for inducting and mentoring new administrators. They select two alternatives for analysis.

The first alternative emphasizes doing as little as possible with formal structure and instead expanding on Don's informal interest in helping beginning school administrators. The idea is to include veteran administrators from inside, and possibly outside, of the district as mentors. The second alternative advocates the establishment of a formal leadership center in the district for the continuing professional development of school principals, central office administrators, and school board members. Part of this approach would be an improved process for the induction of new school administrators. The organization and design of this induction process would be in the hands of the district's cohort of experienced administrators, professors from a local university, and representatives of the school administrators' association in the state. Most groups decide to loosely combine the two alternatives. They suggest implementing the informal system of induction as a low cost first step. Once some experience with this informal approach had been accumulated, the district might be in a position to reconsider the implementation of a formal leadership academy.

Scanning often identifies increased responsibilities for new mentors who are already heavily committed to other activities. Students think that this may result in subsequent inattention to responsibilities or subtle resistance as possible negative consequences. The students propose the development of a pool of volunteers to reduce these negative consequences. They suggest that retired school administrators and retired middle managers and executives from other organizations in the community may help in this capacity. One student suggests, "One of these retired persons might be interested in coordinating the assignment and support of mentors."

Scanning for the second alternative usually causes students to become concerned about the financing of a formal leadership center. The general negative consequence they identify is the possibility that the center will compete with other important programs for limited funds. This situation might result in resistance from those with a stake in these other programs, a comprehensive dilution of program funding in the district, and a reduced cost-benefit ratio for these programs. "If Don moves to the development of a leadership center in the district, he needs to make sure that it is a value-added dimension of the district's programs," notes one student who specializes in school business management. Most students examine fund-raising from foundations or writing proposals for state and federal dollars as ways of reducing the negative consequences. They see the need for someone, perhaps a volunteer, to coordinate this activity with similar efforts by other programs.

More on Teaching Consequence Analysis

Most experienced school principals have been in a situation where a teacher, counselor, or assistant principal has done something that is not necessarily consistent with professional norms, and there is a subsequent complaint against that person from students and/or their parents. For example, consider a complaint against an assistant principal from a student to the principal. On the one hand, assistant principals expect their principal to back them against complaints and criticism from students, even when student complaints have some merit. On the other hand, students expect the principal to right any wrongs done in his or her name. If the principal supports an assistant principal against a student complaint, he or she may risk being seen by students and their parents as unjust or uncaring. If the principal takes the side of the student(s), the assistant principal and some of the faculty may see their superior as unwilling to back the actions of the professional staff. This kind of dilemma occurs in virtually all organizations characterized by hierarchical ordering of roles and social positions, schools are no exception.[12] Consider the following vignette as a possible example of such a dilemma in a middle school.

Denise Twain, principal at Dumas Middle School, is in receipt of a complaint from Sally Sharp's parents. Sally is a fifth-grade student in Alberta Johnson's homeroom. Sally is sometimes an abrasive student who usually earns As and Bs. According to Sally's parents, Johnson overheard Sally using foul language with some other students. She ordered Sally over to a sink and washed Sally's mouth out with soap. After the incident, they claim Sally returned home in tears and phoned them at work.

Both of Sally's parents are school teachers in another district. They report calling Alberta Johnson first to check Sally's story. Apparently, Alberta confirmed the story saying that she had done no more or less than she had done with her own children. They note that they are aware of the respect Johnson has from key community members. However, the parents want Denise to tell them what sort of a learning environment would support such treatment of children. The parents remind Denise of her pledge to parents when she first came to the school as principal: "effective instruction and the humane treatment of children." They warn her that her legitimacy as the instructional leader of the school is on the line with students and parents. Before responding, Denise asks for time to confer with Alberta Johnson to get her side of the story. She promises to call back at the end of the day.

The two meet an hour later. Denise shares her recent conversation with Sally's parents. Alberta replies that she was aware of their concerns because they had called her first. She does not dispute their description of what happened but describes her own behavior as prudent and professional. She claims that mouth washing is well accepted in the community. Denise knows that Alberta is right about the way most parents in the community view the mouth washing practice but expresses serious concern about its use in the teaching profession.

Alberta Johnson shakes her head with disapproval of Denise's concern and says, "Denise, we have a good school here and students respect the authority of teachers. Your predecessor backed his teachers. Since taking the leadership role in this school, you have developed the same reputation. If you take the side of this student and her parents, you will undermine the authority of the entire teaching staff and our trust in you as the leader in this school." She continues, "I am not necessarily saying that I did anything wrong, but if you have any concerns about my behavior, let's talk about them privately and leave our concerns here when we are finished. Above all, let's show a united front in public."

Denise begins to feel uneasy with the conversation because she believes in both backing the faculty and protecting the integrity of the school's learning environment. She can tell from her nonverbal clues that Alberta is anxious. Just as Denise is about to speak, her secretary interrupts, noting that Sally's parents are on the phone.

Backing the professional discretion of teachers, just and humane treatment of students, authentic and honest communications with parents, the integrity of the curriculum and the learning environment are all valued by principals, parents, and teachers alike in virtually every school. These values may seem more difficult to sort through when they are applied to the circumstances described in this case. With this case, we build on the introduction of triad interaction insights from the immediately previous case. Again, the following analysis of a case by a typical group of administration students is presented for descriptive purposes and not as an example of the most appropriate response to the case. We attempt to provide more depth in this next example of how students might draw on selected literature and implement consequence analysis. Furthermore, we make an effort to highlight the likely steps students might take in doing this analysis.

Drawing on Selected Literature

Recalling insights from the course reading list, students might note that schools often exhibit a loosely coupled relationship between administrators and teachers. Because there is no widely accepted work technology of teaching, most teachers prefer and experience relatively high degrees of professional autonomy in their classrooms. Supervision of teaching by administrators tends to be infrequent and done with a gentle touch. Instead, there often exists a "logic of confidence" among teachers and administrators suggesting that teachers hold appropriate degrees and certification, are self-correcting in their work, and therefore, do not require close supervision. This belief is often employed by educators to publicly explain away aberrations in teacher performance and to buffer the school from public criticism.[13]

The instructor might remind students that educators tend to believe in the professionalism of their colleagues and tend to avoid situations where they might observe embarrassing colleague conduct. On the other hand, few believe that teacher misconduct or error should be overlooked by administrators. Teachers may worry that embarrassing teacher lapses might be seen by the public as typical of the entire faculty. Here, saving the face of the entire faculty may take precedence over the face of a single inept or imprudent colleague. Stated another way, teachers know the "rules of the game," they expect one another to abide by them, and principals are expected to step in only when specific teachers exceed the reasonably high thresholds for appropriate behavior.[14]

The administration students suspect that the principal should not necessarily assume that Alberta Johnson's conduct in response to Sally's foul language and abrasiveness will be supported by most or all of the faculty. In the same sense, they suggest that Denise Twain would be ill-advised to assume that Alberta Johnson speaks for all faculty on this matter. Other students note that pupil control norms among teachers and likely parent or community disdain for student misbehavior might not render Sally blameless in this matter.

Focusing on the Presence of a Third Party

As the students begin to speculate about alternative courses of action, the instructor might suggest that the group be careful about alternatives that call for triad interaction, recalling prior class reading assignments. He explains, "Meetings between a superior and a subordinate can take on new dimensions in the presence of a third party. A private conversation between the principal and Mrs. Johnson might be freewheeling and uncensored. The addition of a third party, almost any third party, tends to decrease the openness of communications and strain the emotional ties between the individuals interacting. Comments become formal, guarded, and the minimum required by the circumstances. Given enough time, the interaction will often result in a two against one coalition. Can anyone think of an example?"[15]

The students reflect for a moment, then one says, "Sure, an interaction involving Denise Twain, Alberta Johnson, and Sally puts Sally at a disadvantage. Because she is in the presence of two individuals with considerable authority over her, she might worry that the two would join in a coalition as they address her concerns." The instructor explains, "Knowing this, administrators should not be surprised that students sometimes decide to use their parents as surrogates in advancing their cause. In a meeting with Alberta Johnson and Denise Twain, the presence of Sally's parents might serve as a de facto third party. As such, this new triad may not be any less awkward."

As the students become more familiar with the case, they may relate it to similar experiences they have had or have observed in schools or other organizations. One student might comment, "The dilemma facing the principal, in part, involves avoiding the formation of a damaging two against one coalition. If the principal were to join in a coalition with Sally or her parents, interaction would be strained between this new coalition and Alberta Johnson. Johnson would probably see this as a betrayal on the part of the principal and may take her case to sympathetic others, possibly disrupting professional relationships in the school. If the principal were to support Alberta Johnson, the parents would likely see this as stonewalling their complaint and might take their case to the school board or superintendent, perhaps accompanied by an attorney."

One or two students might add, "The point seems simple and straightforward, no matter which way the coalition develops, one thing is probable: a stressful interaction pattern, negative consequences, and little opportunity for reflection and cooperative problem solving." Another student might reflect out loud about the importance of a vision that might be shared by all parties. The instructor might counsel, as a possibility to consider, "If there is no shared vision, this dilemma may be viewed as an opportunity for faculty members and significant others to reflect about what their school ought to be. Part of this vision might outline how students are to be treated, how student discipline should unfold, the kind of parent-teacher relationships needed, and the principal's desired leadership role." Of course, the instructor's point is that, as noted earlier, dilemmas can be understood by administrators as opportunities for valuation of alternative futures.

Thinking About Vision and Intended Consequences

Let's focus on the work of a single group of students. Their problem definition for this case is, "How can we resolve this conflict in a way that is consistent with the vision for our school?" The problem statement identifies conflict resolution as the primary intended consequence of their work. The vision that has been emerging in this school emphasizes mutual respect among all partners in the school community, partners who learn and grow together. The vision is unfinished, but this initial start has much support. Certainly, this vision has much to contribute to the resolution of the conflict that is unfolding.

Generating Alternatives

The students decide to employ a critical approach to generating alternatives. They identify three possible alternatives. The first alternative would be to have a meeting with Alberta Johnson, Sally's parents, and the principal. The second alternative would be to have two separate meetings, one with Denise Twain and Alberta Johnson, the other with Sally's parents and Denise Twain. Each of these two alternatives would aim for shared decision making and a decision acceptable to all parties. The third alternative is to appoint an impartial committee to investigate and make recommendations to the principal.

Scanning for Negative Consequences

The first alternative was rated least desirable. Using their understanding of third party interaction as a scanning device, this meeting of all three parties identifies a number of negative consequences associated with the development of two against one coalitions. Although it is possible that the negative consequences would not be realized in such meetings, the students decide that the intended consequence of the meeting (resolve the conflict) would hardly be a sure thing. Furthermore, the negative consequences should the principal be forced to decide in favor of one side or the other seemed difficult to reduce or eliminate (alienation of Johnson or Sally's parents).

The students' third alternative, a review by an impartial individual or committee, seemed to be premature. Should more informal steps prove ineffective, this more formal alternative might be invoked as part of due process in a grievance procedure. Schools are dynamic organizations with a number of conflicts of this kind possible at almost any time, setting up a committee for each would seem cumbersome to the professional staff and administrators. This would be particularly true if done without initial attempts by the principal to resolve complaints informally.

Reducing Negative Consequences

Our students decide to use the second alternative, a series of three meetings in dyads, as their approach to solving this problem. In comparison with the other two alternatives, they prefer the fit between the way conflict resolution unfolds in this alternative and the principal's espoused vision for her school. They think that they have a plan for reducing the anticipated negative consequences of this alternative. This plan is thought to be preferable to the efforts that would be required to reduce the respective negative consequences of the other two alternatives. For the most part, the activities for implementing the preferred course of action incorporate those needed to reduce negative consequences.

The students' course of action calls for an initial meeting between Denise Twain and Alberta Johnson. If the first is successful, the second meeting would be between Sally's parents and Denise Twain. In the first meeting, the focus would be on comparing Alberta Johnson's handling of Sally's behavior with other alternatives that might be more consistent with the school vision. Emphasis would be on encouraging Johnson's reflection and professional growth rather than the principal's evaluation, condemnation, and punishment. Recall, the context for this meeting is a dyad not a triad. Interaction would likely be civil and authentic. Also likely would be a number of better alternatives than mouth washing, and possibly some would view the parents as partners rather than adversaries. Furthermore, Johnson might be ready for such reflection in light of her probable observation of a mixed colleague reaction to her behavior or possible civil charges of assault if no constructive action is taken.

With promising and more desirable alternatives to Alberta's previous approach to improving Sally's classroom behavior emerging out of her discussion with Alberta Johnson, the principal would be in a position to become more assertive. The meeting would be behind the scenes and the intended outcome of the meeting would be to reduce teacher reliance on inappropriate approaches by providing new tools consistent with an emerging school vision, tools that the teacher would have a hand in creating and selecting.

Next, Denise Twain would suggest that as principal, she would meet separately with Sally's parents to inform them that Alberta Johnson and she were also unhappy with the consequences of the situation and were exploring other alternatives, possibly more effective ways of responding to Sally's behavior. Emphasis would be on teacher and parents working together to improve Sally's social skills and personal discipline. After all, the central concern of the parents is their daughter's well-being. The principal would encourage both Alberta Johnson, and subsequently, Sally's parents, to meet and discuss Sally's needs further and implement some strategies for working together.

Alberta Johnson might be worried about what Denise Twain might really say about her to Sally's parents. However, if a successful meeting between Johnson and the parents occurs and Sally's behavior improves, the concern is likely to disappear. After Alberta Johnson's meeting with Sally's parents, a brief follow-up by the principal to confirm progress would be in order. If there is no progress, the administration students would implement their third alternative, an impartial third party investigation with a recommended course of action presented to the principal.[16] As one student notes, "Whether the recommendation favors Alberta Johnson or Sally and her parents, such an approach puts the principal in a stronger position to produce a thoughtful response that is both sensitive to the need to provide a fair hearing to all parties and to her espoused school vision."

Additional Thoughts on Teaching Consequence Analysis

After many years of teaching this process, various points are almost sure to arise in activities with students. For example, we are often asked how administrators can be expected to predict or anticipate all negative consequences associated with an alternative. The answer, of course, is that it is unrealistic to seek perfection in this process. Even with the skillful use of an array of scanning frameworks, it is likely that one or more unintended or unanticipated consequences, some negative, will appear during the implementation of the intended problem solution. Although all negatives are unlikely to be identified in advance, understanding this aspect of the process does not absolve a decision maker from the responsibility of making sure that the number of significant unanticipated negative consequences is as small as possible.

A high school principal once told us about his executive committee's interesting use of brainstorming. With a touch of humor and an emphasis on imagination, the committee decided to predict possible but not necessarily probable negative consequences of their already completed plan. When one such unlikely negative consequence actually did appear during implementation, the principal and his committee moved quickly and confidently to implement a rather clever modification. This second level of scanning "for the improbable," led to a teaching exercise that can be used to give students experience with the unintended or unanticipated consequences of a selected course of action. Student groups are asked to exchange their written plans for a particular dilemma. Each group adds negative consequences not anticipated in each of the other plans and returns the augmented plans to the original authors. The groups then work through reducing these new negative consequences by making modifications in their original plan and share their work with one another. The additional negative consequences should be challenging but not impossible to overcome.

We suspect that an administrator's ability to show poise and remain cool and calm under fire is enhanced by the prior understanding that unanticipated negative consequences are always possible (recall Simon's notion of "bounded rationality").[17] Administrators who publicly acknowledge this understanding are less likely to lose face when unanticipated consequences occur. Instead, their occurrence can be met with confidence, patience, and action guided by reflection.

The first time students experience scanning for negative consequences, they sometimes stop after finding what they see as the main drawback to a selected course of action. Of course, scanning should be used to identify as many of the probable negative consequences of a course of action as possible. Usually there are multiple negative consequences for any one course of action. The instructor can encourage students to continue their search for negative consequences by saying, "Are there other negative consequences that you may have overlooked? Why not try one or two other scanning frameworks?" Typically, in their written notes, students list from three to six negative consequences for each proposed course of action.

Another issue that comes up goes something like this, "What is the best way to state a negative consequence?" This question is usually asked after the following interaction between professor and aspiring school administrator. The student reports, "The negative consequence of this alternative is teacher displeasure with the extra paperwork and meetings demanded during implementation." The professor replies, "Resulting in what?" The student usually pauses, looking puzzled because what he thought was obvious is now being challenged. After a few moments of reflection, the student usually suggests, "Well, teachers will probably drag their feet or resist the implementation of the proposed solution." "That sounds right, teacher resistance is the negative consequence," responds the professor. Another student reply might be, "Are you suggesting one best way to state a negative consequence?" The professor responds, "Not necessarily. I find it helpful to insert the phrase 'resulting in' at the end of my statement of a negative consequence. If I find that I have nothing more to add, I feel more comfortable about the statement and leave it as it is. If I can finish my statement with the help of the 'resulting in' phrase, I am usually able to sharpen my focus on the actual negative consequence. This technique seemed to help you get to 'teacher resistance.' This may have been the meaning of your original statement about teacher displeasure over extra work, but why cloak something that can be made clearer?"

A former student who has become a professor of educational administration told us of a visit he made to a sales meeting in a major computer firm's corporate office building. The professor's daughter was a salesperson for the firm and had invited her father to the meeting as a way of familiarizing her parent with the ways of a business organization. Early in the meeting, the sales manager expressed dismay about the way the staff had been completing their travel reimbursement forms. The manager claimed that many of the forms could not be processed because the purpose of the trip was not clear. He stated that company policy required that all travel reimbursed by the company must be directly related to the objectives of each salesperson's annual plan. Unacceptable statements of purpose were "to visit XYZ company, "to follow up on the last visit," and "to make the purchasing agent more aware of our line." The sales manager emphasized the need to identify the intended consequence of the trip. After a while, he became frustrated with his sales persons' confusion about how to complete the form.

Feeling uncomfortable with the rising tensions, the visiting professor hesitantly raised his hand and when recognized, said "I am Fran's dad. I am a professor and this issue comes up occasionally in one of my classes. Why not complete each purpose statement on the form with the phrase 'resulting in' and then finish the sentence?" Everyone seemed surprised at first, but when they tried the idea and it seemed to work, they quickly adopted it and moved on to other business.

Although the cases or vignettes that we have presented are brief, as individuals develop their own cases, they may be as brief as these or as lengthy and in-depth as seems appropriate. To overcome the brevity of the information provided in some of our cases, we find that asking students to develop cases from their own experience (names and places changed to protect identities) can help. If we choose a particular student's case for analysis by the class, the student serves as a consultant to provide additional information on request. The consultant serves as a kind of "human library" of potentially valuable information, serving the same function as the volume of documented information about demographics, personnel, community, and the like that often go with more in-depth case presentations.

So far, much of our discussion has dealt with administrators thinking reflectively about nonroutine problems rather than formal planning activities that involve many persons from the school or school district organization. On the other hand, much of the field testing of this process deals with what we have referred to in earlier chapters as institutionalization, or incorporating consequence analysis into the routine ways that the school organization operates on a daily basis. This early field testing, part of two large funded projects, encouraged principals, teachers, and others to join together as part of a school improvement committee.[18] Working together, they were asked to identify key instructional problems in their school and solutions to those problems. An assessment system, a key dimension of the process, providing a data based aspect to both problem finding and consequence analysis (recall our earlier reference to administrator-originated problems). Delivery of the process was through a statewide network of universities delivering the process to their respective service areas. The building of such networks can be a valuable approach to institutionalizing consequence analysis as a vehicle for enhancing the professional development of teachers, administrators, and professors alike.[19]

Each school improvement committee was guided by monthly objectives that stated desired consequences of the committee's activities. The desired consequences were stated for the following phases of school improvement: organizing the committee for the process, defining a key instructional problem, consequence analysis applied to proposed solutions, and assessing progress toward problem solution. For example, the consequence analysis phase of school improvement targeted the following outcomes or desired consequences for each committee: (a) the committee has scanned the environment for multiple alternative solutions and their consequences; (b) from these, the committee has selected a course of action for field testing; and (c) the committee has developed a plan for reducing negative consequences.[20]

Notes

1. See C. Sargeant and E. Belisle, *Educational Administration: Cases and Concepts* (Boston: Houghton Mifflin, 1955) and J. A. Culbertson, P. B. Jacobson, and T. L. Reller, *Administrative Relations: A Case Book* (Englewood Cliffs, NJ: Prentice Hall, 1960) for early examples of the case method in educational

administration. W. K. Hoy and C. J. Tartar, *Administrators Solving Problems of Practice* (Needham Heights, MA: Allyn & Bacon, 1995) provide a more recent example. J. G. Claudet, "The Value Addedness of Hypermedia as a Pedagogical Learning Tool in Graduate Education Professional Preparation Programs: Preliminary (Phase One) Results of a Longitudinal Study" (paper presented at the annual meeting of the American Educational Research Association, New York, April 1996) presents experiments with interactive cases using hypercard video and CD ROM technology.

2. D. J. Willower, "The Professorship in Educational Administration: A Rationale," in *The Professorship in Educational Administration*, ed. D. J. Willower and J. A. Culbertson (Columbus, OH and University Park, PA: University Council for Educational Administration and The Pennsylvania State University, 1964); J. W. Licata, "Consequence Analysis: Theory and Practice in School Problem Solving," *Educational Technology* 18, no. 9 (1978): 22-28; J. W. Licata and E. C. Ellis, "Utilizing the Georgia Principals' Assessment System as a Resource in Constructing an Instructional Component for School Administrators," *CCBS Notebook* (October, 1976): 5-15.

3. C. D. May, "The Buffalo Returns, This Time as Dinner," *New York Times Magazine*, 26 September 1993; "Back to the Frontier: Buffalo Ranching," *The Economist*, A30, no. 2, 30 April 1994. Also see Mari Sandoz, *The Buffalo Hunters: The Story of the Hide Men* (New York: Hastings House, 1954), 180-81 for a presentation of this hunting method.

4. A. F. Osborn, *Applied Imagination*, 3d ed. (New York: Scribner's), 168.

5. J. P. Guilford, "Creative Thinking and Problem Solving," *The Education Digest* 52 (April, 1964).

6. J. K. Brilhart and L. M. Jochem, "Effects of Different Patterns on Outcomes of Problem-Solving Discussion," *Journal of Applied Psychology* 48, no. 3 (1964): 175-79.

7. Osborn, *Applied Imagination*, 156.

8. See D. J. Willower, "School Reform and Schools as Organizations," *Journal of School Leadership* 1 (1991): 305-15.

9. T. Caplow, *Managing an Organization*, 2d ed. (New York: Holt, Rinehart & Winston, 1983) provides a helpful synthesis of social sciences research on management. The following case draws on his discussion of boundary disputes, managerial indecision as a cause, and reorganization of role and responsibilities as a corrective measure, pages 152-56, and improper coalitions, pages 32-37. Although this case and the case immediately following this one were written by the authors of this book, Caplow's work informed the writing, discussion, and analysis of these cases.

10. Caplow, *Managing an Organization*, 35.

11. The classroom discussion in the last four paragraphs applies Caplow's discussion of the breakdown of cooperation among related departments. See Caplow, *Managing an Organization*, 154.

12. Caplow's review of an alleged persecution of a subordinate by a superior provided a means to build on the study of triads and coalitions in the previous case and inspired our writing of the next case. See Caplow, *Managing an Organization*, 153-54.

13. See K. E. Wieck, "Educational Organizations as Loosely Coupled Systems," *Administrative Science Quarterly* 21, no. 1 (1976): 1-9; J. M. Meyer and B. Rowan, "The Structure of Educational Organizations" in *Environments and Organizations*, ed. M. W. Meyer (San Francisco: Jossey-Bass, 1978), 78-109; J. M. Meyer and B. Rowan, "Institutionalized Organizations: Formal Structure as Myth and Ceremony," *American Journal of Sociology* 83 (1977): 340-63; K. R. Okeafor, J. W. Licata and G. Ecker, "Toward an Operational Definition of the Logic of Confidence," *Journal of Experimental Education* 56, no. 1 (1987): 47-54.

14. The notion of threshold monitors was suggested in D. J. Willower, "School Organizations: Perspectives in Juxtaposition," *Educational Administration Quarterly* 18 (1982): 89-110.

15. This section draws on Caplow's conception of third party presence and the development of two against one coalitions, *Managing an Organization*, 32-35.

16. Caplow, *Managing an Organization*, 153-54.

17. H. A. Simon, *Administrative Behavior* (New York: Macmillan, 1957).

18. The projects referred to are Project ROME-FOCUS, Georgia State Department of Education, the University of Georgia, Valdosta State College and Thomas County Public Schools, 1975-78 and Louisiana LEAD, US Department of Education, Louisiana State University and the Louisiana Department of Education Administrative Leadership Academy in cooperation with nine other universities in Louisiana, 1988-1992.

19. J. W. Licata, "Learner Perceptions of a Clinical Training Component for School Administrators," *Journal of Educational Systems Technology* 9, no. 4 (1980-1981): 55-66 or J. W. Licata and C. D. Ellett, "LEAD Program Provides Support, Development for New Principals," *National Association of Secondary School Principals Bulletin* 74, no. 525 (1990): 5-10.

20. As another example, see J. W. Licata, E. C. Ellis, and C. R. Wilson, "The Principal's Role in Initiating Structure for Educational Change," *NASSP Bulletin* 61, no. 408 (April 1977): 25-33 (reprinted in *Educational Digest* 63, no. 1 [September 1977]: 25-28), for an explanation of the first phase of this process and desired outcomes.

·7·

Additional
Vignettes and Cases

At this point, the reader is invited to take over. Below are a number of cases or dilemmas of practice to use with consequence analysis.[1] As you work through these cases, recall that the purpose of consequence analysis is to identify the alternative with the most desirable intended consequences and whose negative consequences can be most easily reduced or eliminated. In moving toward the identification of such a preferred course of action or problem solution (a) generate multiple alternatives, (b) state each alternative's intended consequences as clearly as possible, (c) use multiple scanning frameworks to systematically identify probable negative consequences, and (d) think through and plan how you might reduce the negative consequences associated with each alternative. Now you are in a position to select a preferred course of action. Recall also that sometimes aspects of two or more alternatives might be combined into an even better course of action.

Occasionally, an instructor will prefer a brief case to emphasize a particular point. To that end, the first three cases are provided. The first case can be used to introduce the concept of valuation, which includes weighing alternatives by their consequences. The second and third cases are opportunities to emphasize the reduction or elimination of anticipated negative consequences to create a viable course of action. The remaining cases present more challenging experiences with consequence analysis.[2]

Case 1

Pioneer Central High School is in an upper-class, suburban school district that takes pride in its crime-free environment. "There is no reason to lock doors or hide valuables here," new students and teachers are told on the first day of school. To help matters, the school administration does a good job with student discipline. They carefully monitor the whereabouts of students with hall passes, enforce tardiness rules, and follow up on absences. The administration supports the faculty, and faculty work together to maintain an orderly learning environment. There are 756 students at Pioneer. They exhibit cooperation and a sense of esprit.

During fourth period, someone entered the boys and girls locker rooms and stole quite a bit of money from the clothing in the lockers. After discovering the loss, both Midge and Foster Thomas, a married couple who teach physical education, report the thefts to Jo Davis, the assistant principal. Jo has had a bad day and, with a sense of defeat, says, "The students are now in their next class, we will never find the thief now. I guess we just need to start locking the locker room doors and the lockers." The two physical education teachers are thoughtful at first, then smile as if offered a welcomed challenge. Midge replies, "Pioneer operates on trust and unlocked doors. No need to change that now." Foster adds, "Locks are no answer. We need to think of an approach that fits Pioneer's way of doing things."

Case 2

Virginia Madison has been a kindergarten teacher at Cairo Elementary School for 1 year. During that year she developed a set of materials and special classroom arrangements she called "the castle of learning." This was her own idea, and much of it was created on her own time. Her classroom looked like a castle. Local storytellers, musicians, and other artists frequented the castle. The PTA provided some funding for this project. Best of all, the system of instruction provided easy planning of daily activities and a regular flow of new ideas. Next year, she thought, would be a breeze.

Due to a large number of second-grade students the following year, Virginia is transferred to a second-grade classroom. Thelma Strong, a veteran teacher, is assigned to her kindergarten classroom. Although Virginia is initially unhappy about the change, she soon decides to simply apply her castle of learning approach to the second grade. The revision of these very familiar materials would not be a big problem. Prior to the first day of school, Virginia visits her former classroom to move her castle set and instructional guide to her new room. Thelma objects by saying, "The materials go with the kindergarten room. They stay right here for my use." Soon both teachers are in the principal's office. Each teacher demands the ownership and use of the castle of learning materials.

Case 3

Sean Spikes is president of the Fair City Board of Education and chairperson of the search for a new school superintendent. The district's population base has become more cosmopolitan over the last 10 years. An unusually diverse group of individuals agreed to serve on the search committee. Two finalists were interviewed for the position: Simon Fuller, an experienced high school principal from a large metropolitan district, and Margo Young, a regional coordinator of special education in the State Department of Education. According to the advertised qualifications for the position, Fuller seemed to have the edge. He impressed the principals in the district and the Chamber of Commerce. Young held appropriate certification but had no district-level administration experience. She has the support of the teachers' association and some influential members of the search committee.

Margo Young emerges as the choice of the search committee by a 7 to 5 vote. She accepts the offer of the Board of Education and will begin in 3 months. The teachers' association is enthusiastic about the hire. The Chamber and the district's corps of administrators are disappointed and some informally question the wisdom of the appointment.

Many of the district's school administration personnel and leaders of the business community feel that the new superintendent lacks the necessary administration experience, and they seem to view her appointment as a statement that their experience is not valued by the community. The teachers' association president, Neal Price, informally characterizes such concerns as "the old boys' lament."

Sean Spikes and the entire Board of Education want the new superintendent to be successful. The Board has asked Sean to meet with the new superintendent and other key opinion leaders to develop some recommendations that would clearly establish their new superintendent as the legitimate leader of the community's educational enterprise and reduce or eliminate potential resistance within the community.

Case 4

Ed Bass is a legend at All Saints College. He is an articulate Civil War historian and head lacrosse coach. There are many stories about Ed that have become part of the saga of All Saints. As one story goes, during the 1960s, when student dissent over Vietnam threatened to put the campus in turmoil, Ed Bass, not the College president, played the key role in avoiding violence and keeping dialogue going with the students. There is a large photograph covering an entire wall in the Student Union of Ed Bass leading a crowd of student protesters in prayer. "The wall" symbolizes the bond that ties each member of the All Saints community together for life. Lacrosse is king at All Saints. Each game is an opportunity to follow Ed's colorful leadership of the team and to celebrate the spirit of All Saints.

Both Ed Bass and the President, Father Boyle, began their careers at All Saints at the same time. They are friends. Father Boyle sometimes jokes privately with Ed that being an ordained minister helps when dealing with coaches who are also campus icons. Over his career, Ed Bass has had trouble controlling his temper while coaching and on two occasions has caused the College considerable public embarrassment. After the last incident, Father Boyle privately warned Ed that one more such incident could very likely endanger his coaching career.

Last week, on ESPN sports television, All Saints faced its traditional nemesis in a game to decide the national championship. In protest of an official's call, Ed loses control and throws equipment from the sidelines all over the field. The officials ask Ed to leave the field. Ed refuses and remains seated on the bench until police escort him off the field. The incident delays the game for 10 minutes and one of the television commentators complains to his national audience, "There is just no excuse for such conduct by Coach Bass. This is not a class act."

Calls flood President Boyle's office the next day. Many are from respected persons not associated with All Saints. They suggest that Bass be removed from his coaching duties. Some loyal All Saints alumni counsel patience and understanding in handling this situation. Faculty and students are saddened by the incident. All await Father Boyle's response.

Case 5

Bill Taylor, age 15, is a ninth-grade student at John F. Kennedy Middle School. Bill has an IQ score of 125. On a statewide achievement test administered at the end of the last school year, Bill scored an 11.3 grade level in reading and a 12.1 in math. His transcripts show that Bill made satisfactory grades in elementary school, but since the sixth grade, his grades have been declining steadily.

Since he entered high school, Bill has been constantly referred to the principal as a discipline problem. His teachers claim that Bill causes many of his own problems by picking on other students. He has been observed chasing other students down the hall, sometimes laughing and sometimes crying. One parent of another boy has complained that Bill is dangerous. His son reports that Bill is constantly threatening to bring a gun to school to "blow some folks away." Bill says that the other boys tease him by stealing his shoes, taunting him, and tearing up his homework. He has publicly threatened to kill them or himself.

In two conferences with the principal, Bill's parents have complained that other students hit Bill while the teachers look on. Bill's father has threatened violence toward any student or teacher who continues to "persecute" his son. He claims that he has a gun and will use it if necessary.

Due to mainstreaming, there is no regular class for exceptional students at John F. Kennedy Middle School. The school counselor conducts a special class weekly, and he has no complaints about

Bill's performance in his class. When Bill returns to regular classes, he has trouble working with his teachers and classmates. His teachers are frustrated about their apparent inability to help Bill.

Because of Bill's husky build, many students have nicknamed him "the whaleman." The nickname was inspired by a unit on *Moby Dick* in English class. The teacher suggested that the whale in this story represented evil. When students see Bill coming down the hall, they taunt him with a chorus of "He-e-e-y Whaleman!" Recently when this happened, Bill threw his backpack at the crowd of students. A student teacher who was nearby had her nose broken by the backpack.

The assistant principal has both the students who instigated the incident and Bill waiting in two different areas. She has also notified the parents of the circumstances. Bill's parents and the parents of the other students blame the principal for not taking action earlier and describe their children's actions as self-defense. Both sets of parents claim they will "fight" any attempt to punish their children. In a telephone conversation, the assistant principal reminds the principal that such an incident would normally call for suspension of Bill and the other students in custody. Furthermore, she notes that the teachers expect a harsh punishment from the principal over the injury to one of their own. She asks the principal, "How should we proceed on this one?"

Case 6

Stewart Landry is completing his second year as principal of a high school in a small city of 15,000 people. Final examinations have been given and report cards have been issued. At about 9:15 in the morning on the day after the last day of school, the secretary informs Stewart that a parent is in the outer office waiting to see him. When Mary Smith, the parent, is ushered into the principal's office, he can see that she is upset. She immediately begins to criticize Fred Brown, a math teacher, who has taught mathematics in this school the past 6 years. Her complaint is that her son, Bobby, had received passing marks on all his algebra tests and on his report cards up to the final examination. On the basis of Bobby's failing grade on the final examination, Fred gave him a failing grade in the course. She complains that Fred was very rude to her when she talked with him on the telephone. She reported that he had said that no one could pass his course who could not pass his final examination.

After hearing Mary's story, the principal assures her that he will discuss the situation with Fred and get back in touch with her during the day. When the meeting takes place, Fred reports that Bobby "earned" an "F" and that, indeed, he told Bobby's mother that no one could pass his course without passing his final examination. He also told her that he thought it had been a mistake for Bobby to have been placed in his algebra course because the boy did not have the ability to handle the course.

When Stewart informs Fred that the records show that he had not always followed this policy, Brown heatedly contends that he had always felt this way but the previous principal had believed in coddling the incompetent and lazy students and had pressured teachers into passing them. He hoped that Stewart would respect the rights of his teachers. Furthermore, he stated that he was disappointed that the principal felt it necessary to pry into the records to find out how he had conducted his classes in the past. It seemed obvious to Fred that Stewart had not supported him against this "unreasonable" parent.

After Fred departs, Stewart sits down to collect his wits. Almost immediately, his secretary reports that Jane Adams, the superintendent, is on the line. After the usual pleasantries, Jane states that a Board of Education member Bob Cain reported that he has been contacted by Bobby's father concerning alleged unfair treatment of his son by Fred. The father claimed that this kind of treatment had happened before and that the school does not need incompetent teachers who don't know how to teach their subjects. Jane asks if it is really true that the boy passed all of the course exams except the final. When Stewart responds positively to this inquiry, Jane expresses disbelief and directs Stewart to bring this case to a satisfactory conclusion.

Case 7

Recently, the new associate superintendent for curriculum met with all of the elementary principals in the school system to announce phase 1 of her plan to implement an outcomes-based curriculum in each elementary school. She seems to have considerable expertise in this area and has written a book and several articles on the subject.

Her plan is to "bring some order out of chaos," as she puts it, by giving more structure to the curriculum. Her plan is to clearly demonstrate to the community that the school system takes accountability seriously.

Jill Sears, a first year elementary principal, has some reservations about this approach to curriculum development because she knows that the autonomy of each teacher in her school has been jealously guarded. However, because the plan has the apparent support of the school board and superintendent, Jill feels that she has little choice but to support the new initiative. After the meeting with the new associate superintendent, Jill puts a memorandum in the mailbox of each of the teachers in her school. The memo states that the associate superintendent will have the responsibility of integrating a new outcomes-based approach with all areas of the regular curriculum. Jill includes a brief description of the associate superintendent's overall plan. She notes the support of the school board and superintendent and calls for cooperation from the faculty.

Just before classes begin the next morning, Mark Jones, a veteran reading teacher, delivers a letter to Jill. He asks Jill to read his letter and notes that he would like to discuss it with her later in the day. Jill recalls that Mark has been employed by the system for 26 or 27 years (long before her time in the profession), teaching almost every subject on every elementary grade level. He has a master's degree in reading and has assumed leadership not only within this school but also in this part of the state. He probably knows more about the inner workings of the school than anyone else on the faculty. Mark is past president of the local classroom teachers association and last year he was named "Teacher of the Year" in the state. His memo follows:

To: Jill Sears
From: Mark Jones

Your memo about the proposed outcomes-based curriculum is causing me great concern and much anguish. In fact, I have been unable to get to sleep because of worrying about this and I am writing this at two in the morning.

Although this plan may look good on paper, you know that the strength of the faculty has always been in its flexibility—which comes from letting each teacher "do his/her own thing." When this new policy takes effect (if it can be called that), it will not only weaken our present ways of assessing student progress but also will lower morale in general. I think I don't need to point out to you that the needs of our school are quite different from other schools in some parts of the city. Also, has it not occurred to you that the role of principal and our total school will lose autonomy to the Central Office? Shouldn't decisions be made by those closest to the task?

Some of the other teachers with whom I talked earlier tonight, have the same concerns and questions. I think that you should persuade the superintendent to rescind this decision. I know the associate superintendent must mean well, but she just doesn't understand the situation here. She needs to know the system and the faculty better before she embarks on any big changes.

Some of the teachers think I should bring our concerns before the executive council of the Classroom Teachers' Association.

During lunch in the teachers lounge, Jill hears several teachers express the same sentiments as Mark. One says angrily, "Outcomes-based? Everything we do is already based on outcomes. What does this new 'expert' think grades and report cards are all about?" Over the next week or so, Jill begins to work with teachers on implementation of the program. She has formed a school steering committee of teachers and parents headed by Mark to do the overall coordination. They have met twice, both meetings lasting well over 3 hours. The last meeting ended with a begrudging endorsement of the plan. One of the committee members, a reporter for the local newspaper, is asked by the committee to prepare a feature story on the school's new initiative. Jill endorses the idea, hoping the new associate superintendent will be pleased by the progress.

At a breakfast meeting the day after the second committee meeting, Kevin Fox, a veteran principal, calls Jill to let her know that the new associate superintendent may have acted prematurely, without the support of the school board and superintendent. He notes that at the Board of Education meeting yesterday, a citizens' "watchdog" group appeared to protest the implementation of an outcomes-based curriculum. They claimed that it would undermine basic family values. The superintendent and board members seemed to be taken aback by the group and claimed no authorization was given for such a program.

According to Kevin, the new associate superintendent was asked to explain this reaction at the meeting. The explanation was along these lines: (a) Outcomes-based curriculum was discussed only as a possibility at the elementary school principals' meeting, and (b) some of the new principals may have misunderstood and been a little overzealous in their initiatives. Kevin warns that the superintendent does not want this incident associated with the central office and appears to be looking for a scapegoat. Jill is stunned; all she can think of is the feature about to appear in today's newspaper about her school's adoption of outcomes-based education. "Kevin, I am new here. Is the local newspaper a morning or evening edition?"

Case 8

During the summer, in an effort to make her English classes more relevant to the world that students might encounter outside the town of Shoreville, Sharon Goodson, an English teacher at McKinley High School, revises her class's reading list. Included on the new reading list are books that have characters from a wide variety of cultures and lifestyles. Finding a need for some additional books in the library, she requests that the school purchase 10 new books. By explaining the plots of each of these books and their part in the year's instructional goals to the principal in a written request, she gains the principal's approval for the purchase.

All appears on track. Students are reading the books on her reading list and discussing the characters and plot development. Some of the books have characters of various cultural backgrounds or ethnicity, some have characters that live in various family arrangements or maintain various lifestyles. These identifications are not a major part of the plot but provide students with a chance to see various kinds of people out of stereotype. This is exactly what Sharon had wanted students to experience, encouraging an unbiased view of the world.

Reverend McCracken, a longtime member of the PTA, discovers Sharon's reading list. He objects to students being provided with reading materials that include characters who are homosexuals or characters who live together out of wedlock. Enlisting the support of certain members of his church that are influential members of the community, they attend a school board meeting and voice their disapproval. The superintendent vows to look into the situation. The next day Reverend McCracken calls the principal who reports that she was aware of the situation and had signed the requisition for the books and the lesson plans. She reports that Sharon is an exceptional teacher with tenure. After the phone conversation, the principal calls Sharon into her office and suggests that Sharon take the books that have the characters in question off the library shelf for the time being.

Sharon says she has a hard time understanding Reverend McCracken's attitude and feels that this matter has been blown out of proportion. The books do not endorse any particular lifestyle but only have characters that happen to lead various lifestyles—much as the other books on the reading list that just so happen to have ethnic characters living in different cultures. The meeting with the principal ends without resolution. Sharon returns to her class and continues teaching from the reading list. The entire faculty strongly supports her position.

The principal is disappointed that Sharon would not give her some time to resolve the problem but respects her professional position on the matter. The superintendent feels the same way. The McCracken complaint is quickly dividing the community and school board right down the middle. The media has decided to run an aspect of the story on a daily basis. Some parents who are fearful of a violent incident, or who are supporters of McCracken, are reporting their children ill and holding them out of school. The superintendent and the president of the school board soon recognize that this situation cannot continue indefinitely. They charge the principal with producing a plan of action.

Case 9

There are two new residents at Willard Hall Hospital, Dr. Vanderhold and Dr. Crowe. Dr. Vanderhold is the niece of John and Mary Vanderhold, who own and operate a network of petrochemical refineries that is the largest employer in the metropolitan area and a provider of approximately one-third of the private endowments for the hospital. She is seen as competent but not outstanding. Her rapport with patients is sometimes compassionate and sometimes very businesslike and cool. On a number of occasions, she has had Dr. Crowe cover for her when she is late or absent as a result of fund-raising work she does with the hospital foundation. A few physicians and nurses think Dr. Vanderhold has taken advantage of Dr. Crowe's willingness to help.

Dr. Crowe comes from a blue-collar family in another city. She is respected by the professional community in the hospital. They think she really cares about her coworkers and her patients. Her performance is seen as competent, and sometimes, very insightful. For instance, she identified a need for a hospice center that would be associated with the hospital. She has been active working for its establishment. During this work, she met her fiancé, a social worker, who has strong ties to the community.

Toward the end of both Vanderhold and Crowe's residencies, the head of the hospital's board of trustees, Truman Turner informs the chief of surgery, Dr. Terry Stanton that there is now funding for the new position Stanton requested for surgery. He states that both Vanderhold and Crowe may be candidates. Of course, he notes, the Vanderhold family is very hopeful that their niece will be the successful candidate. He suggests that there is considerable pressure to fill the position from within. Dr. Stanton states that filling the position from within should be no problem. He notes that although both Crowe and Vanderhold look the same on paper, the hospital's professional community would support Crowe, not Vanderhold, as the best candidate. Truman frowns, "Well, it is your call. Just let me know in advance of your decision."

As expected, both Vanderhold and Crowe apply for the position. Dr. Stanton's consultation with the other surgeons shows strong support for Crowe over Vanderhold. However, they note that they can live with either candidate. Truman Turner calls for an update on the search, suggests a preference for Vanderhold, and ends the conversation by saying again, "Well, it's your call." Then he hastens to add, "But . . . I am worried about the real possibility that the Vanderhold family will reduce their support for the hospital if a decision is made to hire Dr. Crowe over Dr. Vanderhold. We are depending on the Vanderhold family support to finance the new cancer wing for this hospital."

Case 10

Ted Smith is the new principal at Fellowship Christian High School. Mike Lancaster is a veteran teacher in Smith's school. Since his hire 15 years ago, Lancaster has had no additional teacher training. His son is the quarterback on the school's very successful football team. His wife heads the Parent-Teacher Organization for the school. The

Lancaster family has lived in town for generations. Mike and his wife are very popular members of the community. They were instrumental in helping Smith obtain his position.

Mike soon comes to Ted's attention on several occasions. The educational technology director has complained that Mike has continually failed to follow the rules for the proper use of materials and equipment. Because of this behavior, equipment has been destroyed and other teachers were unable to get materials and equipment when they have needed them. The rules and regulations about the use of equipment are spelled out in the teachers' handbook. Mike admits to some of the charges but says they are greatly exaggerated.

Some parents have complained that their children are learning very little in Mike's classes. They report that he shows videotapes almost daily. Sometimes, he will show the same tape 2 or 3 days in succession to the same classes. He has even been accused of showing tapes backward. The day before Christmas vacation, Ted Smith happens to be walking by Mike's classroom and notes that Mike is showing cartoons. Because it is a senior-level mathematics class, Ted Smith discusses this incident with him later in the day. He admits showing movies to the same class twice, showing videotapes backward, and agrees the cartoons had nothing to do with his subject. Repetition, he claims, is useful. Running the movie backward adds humor to the classes, and the last day before vacation seems to call for something such as the cartoons. Ted expresses severe doubts and asks him to reconsider the use of these practices in the future. Subsequent reports from the education technology department indicate he has not followed the new principal's advice.

While making a routine classroom observation in Mike's mathematics class, it was apparent to Smith that his methods are out of date. He used transparencies that were difficult to read and had the students read from a textbook that was also badly out of date. His lesson plan did not coincide with the lesson he was teaching. The plan itself did not describe any purposeful activity. In discussing the lesson with Mike, Ted notes that he did not praise a single student during the entire lesson. Mike seems surprised, then suggests none deserved praise. Smith makes suggestions for improvement, and together Mike and Ted develop a professional development plan. In subsequent classroom visits, Mike seems to be implementing the plan. He has also enrolled in some courses at the university that are part of his plan.

About halfway through the school year, Ted realizes that Mike still needs daily support in the handling of discipline problems. He ranks first among the faculty who make discipline referrals to the office. Many cases involve his claim that students mock him in class. He claims most of his students call him by his first name, and he does not think this is right. Students readily admit that his claims are accurate but complain that he is constantly mocking them and calling them "stupid" or "dummy."

Before the new principal can take further corrective action, a major incident erupts. Parents and students from Mike's senior class come to Ted demanding another teacher. A number of faculty come to his support, claiming that Mike Lancaster is making an effort to improve and they remind Ted that students and parents ought not be in the business of dictating the teaching schedule. Other faculty members claim that the parents' and students' action is hardly in keeping with the school's Christian tradition. Interrupting Ted Smith's choice of a course of action, Mike offers to provide a letter of resignation, he claims that he is doing so because the best interests of the school are far more important than his self-interest. When Ted explains the situation to his superiors on the church council, they describe Mike's offer as unselfish and a commendable example of Christian conduct. They note that Mike Lancaster is a well-respected member of the congregation. Before accepting the resignation, they ask Ted to take his time and be as thoughtful as possible in choosing a course of action.

Notes

1. Most of the case studies (1, 2, 3, 4, 8, and 9) are new, developed specifically for this book. Others (5, 6, 7, and 10) were first written by the Project ROME faculty as a way of teaching consequence analysis to practicing school administrators in Georgia and were recycled years later for use in Louisiana LEAD. Case 6 was contributed to ROME by Elmer Ellis, Associate Director of the project. These ROME cases have been revised a number of times over the years based on extensive field testing in various instructional settings, and they underwent additional revision for use in this book.

2. In addition to providing practice with consequence analysis, we invite the reader to use the case studies as points of reference in developing your own cases.

Index

Activity densities, 48
Administrative work:
  complexities of, 1-5, 21, 41
  everyday tasks of, 21, 28
  pressures of, 1-5
Alexander, J. C., 12
Alternatives, scanning for, 32-34,
  61-62, 69-70, 75-77. *See also*
  Valuation
Altruism, and reflective methods,
  51
Anthropological consequences, 34,
  62
Aristotle, 4, 7-8
Assistant principals. *See* Principals
Assistant superintendents. *See*
  Superintendents

Bentham, J., 8
Bias, in science, 18-19

Boards of education, in cases:
  on outcomes-based curriculum,
    92
  on superintendent
    qualifications, 85-86
Brainstorming, for alternatives,
  60-61, 77-78
Budgeting, case on, 58-60
Buffalo herd instinct, case on,
  57-58

Case method, of teaching, 55-80
Cases:
  brief, 63, 84-86
  developed by students, 79
  on an exceptional student, 87-88
  on coach's temper, 86-87
  on funds distribution, 58-59
  on grading policy, 88-89
  on herd instinct, 57-58

CORWIN
PRESS

The Corwin Press logo—a raven striding across an open book—represents the happy union of courage and learning. We are a professional-level publisher of books and journals for K-12 educators, and we are committed to creating and providing resources that embody these qualities. Corwin's motto is "Success for All Learners."